U.S. Citizen, *yes*

Preparing for Citizenship

3rd Edition

Barbara Grubb
919-538-4120
grubbstudents@
gmail.com

Anne Tekmen
eatekmen@
waketech.edu
(919) 334-1546

Ronna Magy

HEINLE
CENGAGE Learning

Australia • Brazil • Japan • Korea • Mexico • Singapore • Spain • United Kingdom • United States

**U.S. Citizen, Yes: Preparing for Citizenship
3rd Edition**

Ronna Magy

Pulisher: Sherrise Roehr

Aquisitions Editor: Tom Jefferies

Assistant Editor: Cécile Bruso Engeln

Director of US Marketing: Jim McDonough

Marketing Manager: Caitlin Driscoll

Content Project Manager: John Sarantakis

Print Buyer: Betsy Donaghey

Interior Designer: Silber Design

Compositor: Integra

Illustrator: Ray Loft/Scott MacNeill

Cover Designer: The Creative Source

For product information and technology assistance, contact us at
Cengage Learning Customer & Sales Support, 1-800-354-9706

For permission to use material from this text or product,
submit all requests online at **www.cengage.com/permissions**
Further permissions questions can be emailed to
permissionrequest@cengage.com

Library of Congress Control Number: 2008942276

ISBN-13: 978-1-4240-9599-5

ISBN-10: 1-4240-9599-9

Heinle
20 Channel Center
Boston, MA 02210
USA

Cengage Learning is a leading provider of customized learning solutions with office locations around the globe, including Singapore, the United Kingdom, Australia, Mexico, Brazil, and Japan. Locate your local office at: **www.cengage.com/global**

Cengage Learning products are represented in Canada by Nelson Education, Ltd.

Visit Heinle online at **elt.heinle.com**

Visit our corporate website at **www.cengage.com**

Printed in Canada
2 3 4 5 6 7 8 9 10-13 12 11 10 09

Table of Contents

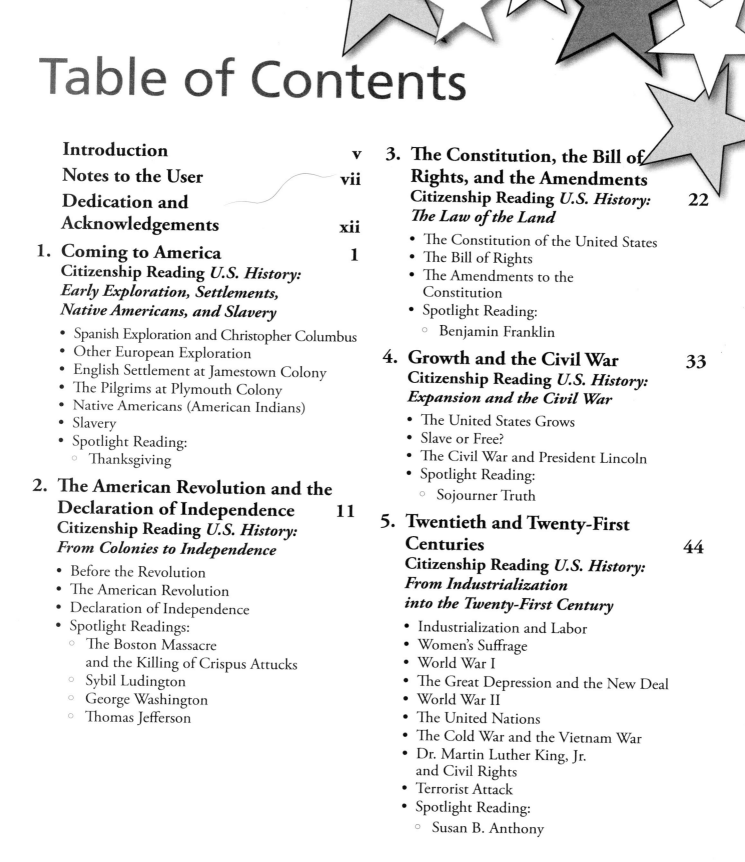

Introduction

U.S. Citizen, Yes, Third Edition is designed to prepare beginning and intermediate level adult students of Citizenship and English as a Second Language for the naturalization process. The book consists of ten units that present the content a student is required to learn to become a citizen of the United States. Activities in ***U.S. Citizen, Yes*** encourage students to talk and interact in pairs and groups. The book builds on students' life skills and knowledge while encouraging them to compare life in the United States with the life, history, and government of their native countries.

New features in the third edition include:

- ★ **Unit Focus** page at the beginning of each unit establishes the unit theme
- ★ **Key Vocabulary Preview** sections at the beginning of each unit focus on key words
- ★ **Spotlight Readings** highlight important historical figures, events, and U.S. landmarks
- ★ Expanded **Take the Test** sections giving additional test taking practice
- ★ **Community and Civics Participation Projects** provide ideas for ways students can learn about and take part in community, local, state, and national events
- ★ Audio CD practice with **Take the (Oral) Test** provides students additional question and answer practice with the 100 questions, the USCIS Civics (History and Government) Items for the Naturalization Test
- ★ Audio CD dictation practice with the USCIS *Writing Vocabulary* words creates opportunities for sentence writing practice

Beginning Level pages 114 to 125 invite lower-level students to learn about citizenship. These visually rich pages familiarize the students with the content of U.S. history, government, and civics in a nonthreatening format so that they can more easily access the naturalization information in the rest of the book.

The first five units of ***U.S. Citizen, Yes*** cover U.S. history: explorers and colonization, the American Revolution and the Declaration of Independence, the Constitution and the Bill of Rights, the 1800s and the Civil War, and the twentieth and twenty-first centuries. The last five units cover the symbols, songs, and celebrations of the United States; the legislative, executive, and judicial branches; state and local government; and the final interview with the U.S. Citizenship and Immigration Services (USCIS).

In the text, essential information on U.S. history, government, and civics is integrated with the skills of listening, speaking, reading, and writing in English. Every unit includes a practice test with multiple-choice, dictation, and interview questions to familiarize students with the USCIS testing procedures. With the third edition, the multiple-choice and dictation test questions can also be easily accessed and practiced using the audio CD.

Throughout the book, clarification strategies have been introduced to help students during their interviews. Asking for clarification, asking for repetition, checking for understanding, and using questioning strategies will assist student applicants with the interview process.

Included in Appendix B are the 100 USCIS questions and answers. The USCIS N-400 Form (Application for Naturalization Form) in Appendix B can be used for student practice. The **Community and Civics Participation Projects** provide students with opportunities for the real life application of historical lessons.

The theme-based units begin with lively and interactive pre-reading activities. Beginning with key vocabulary words, students and their instructor participate actively in these individual, pair, group, and whole-class activities. A class brainstorm from focus words leads students into the **Citizenship Reading**. From the reading, students create, review, and expand their personal dictionaries of key vocabulary words. Post-reading activities include a comprehension check and vocabulary review. Timelines are presented through the book to help students sequence and put events into historical context. **Spotlight Readings** give students a more in-depth knowledge of the events, people, and places that make up U.S. history. A role play leads students off the printed page and into historical reality.

Interview questions and personal stories written by other students act as springboards to suggested writing topics. Multiple-choice test questions, USCIS interview questions, and dictations prepare students for the Naturalization Test. Each unit ends with a board game that reviews the content of the lesson and encourages lively interactivity.

Notes to the User

To The Teacher

Below are suggestions for using and enhancing the activities in the third edition of *U.S. Citizen, Yes.* Included are individual, pair, small group, team and whole class activities.

Unit Focus and Key Vocabulary Preview

The initial unit page establishes the unit theme and previews important vocabulary words and phrases. Use the picture on the unit opener page (an important document, person, historical landmark, or map) to lead students into a discussion of the unit theme. (These discussions will activate students' background knowledge and generate whole class involvement.)

★ **Document** *What is this document? What do you know about it? What are the important words in this document? When was it written? What did this document do to change the history of the United States? Is there a document like this in the history of your country?*

★ **Person** *Who is the person you see in the picture? What did he or she do that changed the history of the United States? When did he or she live? Is there a person like this in the history of your country?*

★ **Landmark** *What is the name of this object/statue/building? When was it built? What does it represent? What are important facts about this object/statue/building? Is there a(n) object/statue/building like this in your country?*

★ **U.S. Map** *What country do you see? Where is our state? What states are to the north, south, east, and west of this state? Is this state to the east or west of the Mississippi River? Is this state to the east or west of the Missouri River? Who is the governor of this state?*

Use the information students generate and build on it. *That's right, it's the Statue of Liberty. Do you know where the Statue of Liberty is located? What country gave the Statue of Liberty to the United States? When?*

1. Before You Read

Pre-reading activities provide learners additional opportunities to activate their prior knowledge and voice ideas and opinions. Relying on their own experience and life skills, students generate words and ideas about the unit theme in three general types of activities.

A. **Discussing** With a partner or in a small group, students ask and answer questions about the unit theme. Here is one way this can be done in a group: Student A asks Student B the first question. Student B answers. Student B then asks Student C the first question. Student C answers. The process continues until all the group members have asked and answered the question. The same procedure is used for the remaining questions.

B. **Creating Charts** Working with charts is a useful skill in academic and work-related environments. Students create charts using information they get from their peers. Students sit in groups of four. The teacher or the group selects a group leader. The leader asks the other three students the questions from the chart. One group member then asks the leader the questions. Students summarize the information about their groups.

C. **Reporting** Student groups share summarized information and ideas with their classmates. Summarizing helps develop a feeling of class community, allowing students to see what they have in common and to see what makes each of them unique. *Three students in our group are from Mexico. Two students in our group came to the United States by plane.* The teacher may ask the class members to record the new information in their books.

Extension Activities

★ The teacher hangs large pieces of paper in different areas of the room and lists the words or ideas generated by the **Unit Focus** and **Before You Read** sections. Students write additional word associations on the paper with crayons or magic markers.

EXAMPLE OF IDEA: war
EXAMPLE OF WORD ASSOCIATION: winning, death, soldiers

★ Report Back Chart: As the groups creating charts report back to the class, the teacher or a student creates a chart on the board that consolidates the information from the different groups. Using the chart on the board, class members summarize and write sentences.

EXAMPLE OF CLASS INFORMATION: *Twelve people from our class came to the United States by car.*

★ Class Mixer: Students walk around the classroom reporting what they learned about their classmates. Student A says, *Did you know that twelve people from our class came to the United States by car?* Student B says, *Really? I didn't know!* Student B adds, *And did you know that ten people came from Africa?* Student A comments, *How interesting!*

★ Brainstorm Preview Questions: In groups of four, students brainstorm questions for ten minutes on one **Unit Focus** theme or the **Before You Read** topic. Then two groups work together. Each student selects a question and poses the question to someone from the other group.

2. Citizenship Reading

Specific citizenship information correlated to the USCIS questions is provided in the main reading selections.

A. **Thinking about Key Words** Two to three key words and ideas are presented in this section of each unit. Together with classmates, students brainstorm word associations with the key words. With their teacher, they preview and predict the content material in the readings.

B. **Working with Timelines** The timelines that precede the **Citizenship Readings** can be used to predict content information. Students ask each other *when* or *where* questions about the timelines.

EXAMPLE: *When did the Pilgrims land at Plymouth, Massachusetts?*

C. **Readings** After the word-association brainstorm, students discuss the subheadings, the diagrams, and the pictures in each reading. The teacher reads a section to the class and then leads a discussion about it. Students may want to ask questions about the material, discuss vocabulary words in context, read the section with a partner, or read the section silently. The teacher asks specific content-review questions.

D. Creating a Student Dictionary In each unit, the **Key Vocabulary Preview** and **Citizenship Readings** will introduce students to new words. Have students create a student dictionary for personal reference, using a notebook to record the words.

As students reread the text, ask them to circle new vocabulary words. They then share these words with the teacher, who lists them on the board. The teacher explains each word, giving examples and a definition that students record in their dictionaries. Students then practice the definitions with one another.

EXAMPLE: What is a *colony*?

With a partner, students brainstorm and write a sentence to go with each word.

Extension Activities

★ Learners sit in a group of four. Each student selects two new vocabulary words from the reading and writes each word on a separate piece of paper. All eight papers are put in a pile. One person from the group draws a word. The person says the word and what he or she thinks the word means. If necessary, the group helps the student formulate a definition. The person (with the assistance of the group) puts the word in a sentence or reads a sentence from the text that contains the word. Other group members copy the sentence into their student dictionaries.

★ Learners write each event or date from the timeline on separate pieces of paper and put them in a bag. Each learner then draws a piece of paper out of the bag and gives the date for the event, or an event for the date.

★ The teacher divides the class into two teams, writes events from the timeline on separate pieces of paper, and puts the pieces of paper in a bag. Each student on one team draws an event from the bag. Then, all the students on the team line up in front of the class in the correct chronological order of the events they have drawn. The other team checks their accuracy.

★ Students compare the timeline to events in their native countries during the same time period.

3. After You Read

Post-reading activities provide learners the opportunity to check for comprehension of the content material and vocabulary words. These activities encourage students to return to the reading to review the meaning of vocabulary words and check for information. They also help students acquire essential information in a low-stress, high-success environment.

Extension Activities

★ In pairs or small groups, students write *what, where, when, why,* and *how* questions about the information in the **Citizenship Reading**. Using the questions, they quiz each other on the content.

★ Students discuss historical events in their own countries and the events in each unit: revolution, civil war, times of economic depression, etc.

4. Spotlight Readings

These short readings highlight biographies of important historical figures, events in U.S. history, and significant landmarks which provide students with additional knowledge of the depth and texture of U.S. history and government. From Benjamin Franklin to Susan B. Anthony, from the Statue of Liberty to the Capitol Building, students get a taste of the "real" people and places of the United States.

Extension Activities

★ In pairs, students compose *what, where, when, why,* and *how* questions about the information in the **Spotlight Reading**. Using the questions they have composed, pairs interview another pair of students.

★ Students go online to find additional information on the people, places, and events highlighted in the spotlight readings. They compose reports and present the information to the class.

5. Make It Real

Drama and role play can help bring the content of each chapter to life. Students form groups of four. Each group picks one of two scenes. Acting as the characters in the scene, learners discuss the issue for ten minutes. Representatives of the two groups meet to talk about the issue.

NOTE: Some students find it easier to role play than others. The following questions can be asked by the teacher to assist students in the role play:
What do you think these people looked and dressed like at the time? What did they eat? What did they think about? What did they talk about?

6. Real Stories

Reading authentic student stories can stimulate learners to write their own personal stories. The following procedure is suggested.

A. **Reading** Focusing on the photograph of the student writer and the story title, students predict what the story is about. Then they read the story and tell a partner what they liked about it.

B. **Discussing and Writing** With a partner, students talk about the guided questions. These questions are intended to connect the story to students' personal experiences. After a discussion, students are ready to write their own personal stories. Finally, each student reads his or her story to a partner, and the partner asks a question about the story.

Extension Activities

★ Learners work cooperatively in pairs to revise their personal stories.

★ Learners make a class book of student writing for each topic. The book becomes an anthology for class members to read and reread.

7. Take the Test

These activities prepare students for the citizenship test and the USCIS interview by giving them practice with the specific questions that may be asked. Multiple-choice, dictation, and interview questions are included. The **Clarification Section** helps students to request, with confidence, repetition and clarification of information during the interview.

8. Think About Your Learning

Students reflect on and begin taking responsibility for their learning by choosing their favorite activity and circling what they want to study more about.

9. Games

Reviewing the unit content in a playful, nonthreatening situation will help students internalize key facts. For this activity, each group of four will need a die and the game board from the unit, and each student will need a marker (a coin, a paper clip, or a pencil eraser). Students throw the die, move their markers around the game board, answer the questions they land on, and review the material in the unit. If a student does not know the answer to a question, he or she goes back to her or his previous square. If a student lands on a picture square, no question is asked and he or she remains there until the next turn. The teacher facilitates the game by answering questions and settling disputes.

After all the groups have played the game once and are familiar with the questions and answers, two students from each group move to a different group and the new groups play the game again.

Dedication and Acknowledgements

For Esther and Irvin Magy, Stu and Arlen Magy, Minnie Hutton, Helen Rachinsky, Gert Levine, Inez Aidlin, and Francis Eisenberg.

To all the students who shared their stories of coming to the United States.

To my editors, Tom Jefferies and Cécile Bruso Engeln, who saw me through this process, and to the following faculty and staff:

Ed Morris *Los Angeles Unified School District Division of Adult and Career Education*

Kit Bell *Los Angeles Unified School District Division of Adult and Career Education*

Nancy Agabian *City University of New York Queens College*

Jolie Bechet *Westside Community Adult School*

Rodney Borr, Julie Singer *Garfield Education and Career Center*

Greg Dobie, Gwen Mayer, Marna Shulberg *Van Nuys Community Adult School*

Jill Gluck *Hollywood Community Adult School*

Thelma Gonzalez, Victor Huey, Arcides Martinez, Susan Ritter, Ethel Watson *Evans Community Adult School*

Barbara Hughes *South Gate Community Adult School*

Irene Katsui, Portia La Ferla, Debby Phillips *Torrance Unified School District*

Liz Koenig *Pierce College, Los Angeles Unified School District Division of Adult and Career Education*

Angela Locke *Santa Barbara City College Adult and Continuing Education*

Timothy McAleer, Deborah Thompson *El Camino Real Community Adult School*

Jean Owensby *Harbor Community Adult School, Los Angeles Unified School District Division of Adult and Career Education*

Lynn Thompson *Gardena Community Adult School*

Arlene Torluemke *Los Angeles Unified School District Division of Adult and Career Education*

A special thank you to Joan, Sylvia, Steve, Arlene, Barry, Dave, and Elizabeth for all their understanding and support.

Unit 1
Coming to America

Samoset Bids Pilgrims Welcome

Unit Focus

☆ Spanish Exploration and Christopher Columbus

☆ Other European Exploration

☆ English Settlement at Jamestown Colony

☆ The Pilgrims at Plymouth Colony

☆ Native Americans (American Indians)

☆ Slavery

☆ Spotlight Reading: Thanksgiving

Key Vocabulary Preview

Christopher Columbus
missions
Mayflower
economic opportunity
slavery

Native Americans
America
Thanksgiving
colonies

American Indians
Europeans
freedom
African slaves

Spanish
Pilgrims
religious freedom
Africans

1. Before You Read

A. Sit in a group of four. Look at the world map on page 153. Draw a line from your native country to the place where you live now. Do the same for your classmates.

B. Find out about the members of your group. Ask these questions. Fill in the chart.
   1. What's your name?
   2. What country are you from?
   3. When did you come to the United States?
   4. How did you come to the United States? (walk, bus, car, train, boat, plane, etc.)

Name	Country	When	How
Elena	El Salvador	1987	plane and car

C. Tell your class about one student in your group.

   EXAMPLE: Elena is from El Salvador. She came to the United States in 1987. She came by plane and car.

2. Citizenship Reading

A. What do you know about these words? Write your ideas on the lines.

Columbus   Pilgrims

B. Read.

U.S. History: Early Exploration, Settlements, Native Americans, and Slavery

Columbus lands on San Salvador		British colonists settle at Jamestown		Pilgrims settle at Plymouth
1492	**1519**	**1607**	**1619**	**1620**
	Cortés invades Mexico		Spanish build mission at San Geronimo (now New Mexico)	

Spanish Exploration: Columbus   Christopher Columbus was an explorer and trader. He was looking for a new way to India. He was looking for spices, silk, and gold. Queen Isabella and King Ferdinand of Spain paid for his trip. Columbus and his crew sailed across the Atlantic Ocean on three ships—the *Niña*, the *Pinta*, and the *Santa María*. In 1492, they landed on an island in the Caribbean Sea. They named the island San Salvador. Because he was looking for India, Columbus named the Native Americans he saw *indios*, or Indians. Europeans called the place where Columbus landed the New World.

Other European Exploration   In 1519, Hernán Cortés invaded and conquered the Aztec city of Tenochtitlán, now called Mexico City. After Cortés, Spanish explorers Francisco Vásquez de Coronado and Hernando de Soto came to what is now New Mexico looking for gold and silver. In 1619, the Spanish built a mission at San Geronimo in what is now New Mexico. The Spanish built other missions in California, Texas, and New Mexico. They wanted to convert the native peoples to Christianity.

After Columbus, other explorers from England, France, Holland, Spain, and Portugal traveled to the Americas. Some explorers became rich from the furs, fish, gold, silver, and land they took from the Native Americans (American Indians). Many colonists forced the Native Americans (American Indians) to work on farms and in mines. Many Native Americans developed serious diseases and died from contact with the explorers. The Native Americans tried to fight against the Europeans, but the Europeans' guns were stronger.

English Settlement at Jamestown Colony   In 1607, English settlers were sent by the Virginia Company to begin a trading post in America. They came to America for economic opportunity and freedom. They landed near Chesapeake Bay, Virginia. They established the first English colony at Jamestown, named after King James of England.

Algonquin Indians in the 1600's

Pilgrims

Winters were very cold in Virginia and the settlers had no food. Sometimes they ate dogs, rats, and mice to survive. Unfortunately, many early Jamestown colonists died of hunger, disease, and cold, but the colony of Jamestown survived.

The Pilgrims at Plymouth Colony   The Pilgrims were a part of a religious group that wanted freedom from the Church of England. They left England in 1620 and sailed to North America looking for religious freedom. They sailed on the ship called the *Mayflower*. The Pilgrims wanted to go to Virginia, but the *Mayflower* landed at Plymouth, Massachusetts. The weather in the winter of 1620 was very cold and often the Pilgrims had no food. One half of the Pilgrims died that winter. In 1621, the Native Americans taught the Pilgrims how to survive by planting, fishing, hunting, and building houses.

After their first harvest in 1621, the Pilgrims celebrated Thanksgiving with the Native Americans. They wanted to thank God for their food and their new lives. Now, we celebrate Thanksgiving on the fourth Thursday in November. On Thanksgiving, some traditional foods we eat are turkey, stuffing, corn, and pumpkin pie.

Native Americans   The Native Americans are the indigenous peoples of the Americas. They were living on the lands of the Americas for thousands of years before Columbus arrived. In the area that is now the United States, some of the Native American (American Indian) tribes are the Algonquin, Cherokee, Navajo, Sioux, Chippewa, Choctaw, Pueblo, Apache, Iroquois, Creek, Blackfeet, Seminole, Cheyenne, Arawak, Shawnee, Mohegan, Huron, Oneida, Lakota, Crow, Teton, Hopi, and Inuit.

Slavery in the Colonies   There were both African and Native American (American Indian) slaves in the colonies. From the 1600s through the 1860s, people from different African countries were forced to come to the United States as slaves. In Africa, they were free. They were bought in Africa and brought over by slave traders. Conditions on slave ships were terrible. Slaves were chained together so they could not move. There was little food and water, so many slaves became sick and died.

After they arrived in the colonies, slaves were bought and sold by slave traders or their representatives. Some Europeans living in the colonies had slaves. Most slaves in the colonies worked on plantations or as domestic servants.

C. Review the reading. Circle any new words. Begin making your own dictionary of new vocabulary words. Discuss the new words with your teacher and classmates.

3. After You Read

A. Read the sentences. Put a ✔ in the correct column. You may check more than one column.

1. Who looked for a new route to India?
2. Who sailed across the Atlantic Ocean?
3. Who came for religious freedom?
4. Who was looking for spices, silk, and gold?
5. Who sailed on the *Mayflower*?
6. Who did the Native Americans (American Indians) teach to survive in America?

	Columbus	Pilgrims
1.	✔	
2.		
3.		
4.		
5.		
6.		

B. Fill in the blanks with the words below. Read the story with a classmate.

landed	Indians	*Mayflower*	colony
religious freedom	died	Thanksgiving	missions
Pilgrims	~~India~~	Africans	slaves

In 1492, Columbus was looking for (1) _____India_____ . His ships,

the *Niña,* the *Pinta,* and the *Santa María,* (2) _____ at

San Salvador Island. Columbus named the Native Americans he met *indios,* or

(3) _____ .

Jamestown was the first English (4) _____ in North America.

Many Jamestown colonists (5) _____ because there was no food and

the weather was cold.

Spanish explorers came to North America in the 1500s. The Spanish built

(6) _____ in California, Texas, and New Mexico.

The (7) _____ came to America from England. They wanted to

have (8) _____ _____ . They sailed on the

(9) _____ . The ship landed at Plymouth, Massachusetts. Living in a

new country was difficult for the Pilgrims. The Native Americans (American Indians) showed

the Pilgrims how to plant, hunt, fish, and build houses. In 1621, the Pilgrims and Native

Americans (American Indians) celebrated the first (10) _____ .

(11) _____ were taken to America and sold as slaves. Most

(12) _____ were forced to work on plantations or as domestic

servants.

4. Spotlight Reading

Thanksgiving

In the United States, people celebrate Thanksgiving Day on the fourth Thursday in November. On Thanksgiving, we remember the history of the Pilgrims and the Native Americans (American Indians). We eat special foods like turkey, sweet potatoes, and pumpkin pie. We celebrate the holiday with family and friends.

In September 1620, one hundred Pilgrims and workers left England on the *Mayflower*. The Pilgrims left England looking for religious freedom. The Pilgrims wanted to go to Virginia, but they arrived in Massachusetts. In December 1620, the *Mayflower* landed at Plymouth Rock in Massachusetts.

The first winter in Plymouth Colony was freezing. Half of the colonists were sick and died. In the spring, the Native Americans (American Indians) helped the colonists to plant crops, fish, hunt, and survive in the new land. In the fall of 1621, the Pilgrims had a good harvest. The Pilgrims invited the Native Americans (American Indians), led by Chief Massasoit, to share their food. Fifty Pilgrims and ninety Native Americans (American Indians) celebrated the first Thanksgiving.

Now, Thanksgiving is a national holiday. On Thanksgiving Day, people give thanks for all the good things in their lives. They remember the history of the Pilgrims and the Native Americans.

5. Make It Real

A. Sit in a group of four. Read the scenes below. Talk in your group about one of the scenes.

Scene 1	Scene 2
Imagine you are a Native American. You see the Pilgrims arrive at Plymouth, Massachusetts. Talk about how you feel. One group member writes the ideas.	Imagine you are a Pilgrim. It is the spring of 1621. Many of your people have died. Some Native Americans come to help you. Talk about how you feel. One group member writes the ideas.

B. Now, meet a student from another group—either a Pilgrim or a Native American. Introduce yourself. Talk about your feelings toward the other group. Talk about your future. Talk about your past.

6. **Real Stories**

A. Read a student's story.

Memories of a Homeland

My hometown, Jiyoung, South Korea, was famous for sweet persimmons. Most mountains in the area were used as persimmon farms. The color of the mountains was different in every season. From late October to mid-November, the mountains were scarlet, the same color as persimmons. In that season, all the leaves fell off the trees. Only the fruit was hanging from the branches. In the spring, persimmon leaves and flowers made the mountains change to green and white. During that season, children made flower chains with the leaves. In the winter, the mountains looked dark and scary. Why? The thin black branches of the persimmon trees made people, especially little children, feel afraid.

Hyun Jung Lee

B. Talk to a classmate about this question:

What are some things you remember from your native country?
- ★ Things you liked to look at
- ★ Things you liked to smell
- ★ Things you liked to do

C. Write a story about some things you remember from your native country.

_____

_____

_____

_____

_____

_____

D. Read your story to a partner. Ask your partner a question about his or her story.

7. Take the Test

This section will give you practice for the Naturalization Test.

CD 1
Track 1

A. Listen to the questions. Circle the correct answers.

1. Who lived in America before the Europeans arrived?
   - **a.** Queen Isabella and King Ferdinand
   - **b.** the American Indians (Native Americans)
   - **c.** King George III
   - **d.** George Washington

2. Why did colonists come to America?
   - **a.** to look for gold
   - **b.** to go to India
   - **c.** to buy tea
   - **d.** for religious freedom and economic opportunity

3. Who helped the Pilgrims in America?
   - **a.** Columbus
   - **b.** the Native Americans (American Indians)
   - **c.** Plymouth
   - **d.** the *Mayflower*

4. What was the name of the Pilgrims' ship?
   - **a.** Thanksgiving
   - **b.** Plymouth
   - **c.** the *Santa María*
   - **d.** the *Mayflower*

5. What holiday was celebrated for the first time by the American colonists?
   - **a.** Halloween
   - **b.** Thanksgiving
   - **c.** Christmas
   - **d.** New Year's Eve

6. Name two American Indian (Native American) tribes in the United States.
   - **a.** England and France
   - **b.** Holland and Portugal
   - **c.** *Niña* and *Pinta*
   - **d.** the Iroquois and the Algonquin

7. Africans were brought to America and sold as _____ .
   - **a.** free
   - **b.** slaves
   - **c.** colonists
   - **d.** Pilgrims

B. Now, listen again and check your answers.
Review the questions and answers with your partner. (Answers are at the back of the book on page 155.)

C. Listen to each sentence. Then, listen again and write what you hear.

1. _____

2. _____

3. _____

4. _____

Pairs: Check your partner's answers with the sentences on page 155.

D. N-400 Parts 1, 3, and 4: Your Name, Address, and Eligibility Interview a partner. (See pages 106–110 in Unit 10 for additional questions.)

1. What's your first name?
2. What's your last name?
3. What's your address?
4. What's your telephone number?
5. What's your birth date?
6. What's your USCIS "A" number?
7. How long have you been a Lawful Permanent Resident of the United States?

E. Clarification: If you don't understand something in the interview, you can say: *I'm sorry. I don't understand your question.*

8. **Think About Your Learning**

My favorite activity in this unit was _____ .
I want to study more about:
❒ Native Americans
❒ Columbus
❒ Spanish and other European Explorers
❒ Jamestown Colony
❒ Pilgrims
❒ Slavery
❒ _____ (other)

9. Game

	What year was the first Thanksgiving? →	What are some traditional Thanksgiving foods?	When is Thanksgiving celebrated in the United States?	FINISH ★ ★ ★
Who helped the Pilgrims hunt, fish, plant, and build houses? ↑	Where did the Mayflower land?	Where did the Pilgrims want to go?	Why did the Pilgrims come to America?	What country did the Pilgrims come from? ← ↑
Name three American Indian tribes. ↑	Why did the colonists come to America? →		What year did the Pilgrims come to America?	How did the Pilgrims come to America?
Who lived in America before the Europeans came?	What did Europeans call America?	Africans were brought to America and sold as _____.	What things was Columbus looking for?	What did Columbus name the Native Americans? ← ↑
START ★ ★ ★ →	Who was Colombus?	What country was Colombus looking for?	What were the names of the ships?	Where did Columbus and his crew land?

Unit 2
The American Revolution and the Declaration of Independence

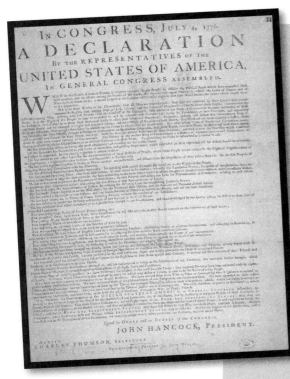

The Declaration of Independence

Unit Focus

☆ Before the Revolution

☆ The American Revolution (1775–1783)

☆ Declaration of Independence (July 4, 1776)

☆ Spotlight Readings:
The Boston Massacre
  and the Killing of Crispus Attucks
Sybil Ludington
George Washington
Thomas Jefferson

Key Vocabulary Preview

colonies	Boston Massacre	George Washington	Declaration of Independence
colonists	Crispus Attucks	president	equal rights
government	Boston Tea Party	"Father of Our Country"	life, liberty
Great Britain (England)	American Revolution	commander in chief	Independence Day
soldiers	Revolutionary War	United States	July 4, 1776
Patrick Henry			Thomas Jefferson

1. Before You Read

A. Sit in a group of four. Look at the picture above. Talk about the questions.
   1. Why did you leave your country? (war, no jobs, money, political problems, etc.)
   2. Who did you leave behind in your country?
   3. Why did you decide to come to the United States?

B. Discuss these questions with your group. Write your answers in the chart.

What are some important things you brought with you from your country?

EXAMPLES: photos, marriage certificate

What are some ideas you brought with you from your country?

EXAMPLES: work hard, save money

Things	Ideas
photos, marriage certificate	work hard, save money

C. Read your group's list to the class. Listen to other groups as they read their lists. Write any new ideas on this page.

2. Citizenship Reading

A. What do you know about these words? Write your ideas on the lines.

American Revolution

Declaration of Independence

B. Read.

U.S. History: From Colonies to Independence

Boston Massacre		Revolutionary War begins		Revolutionary War ends
1770	**1773**	**1775**	**1776**	**1783**
	Boston Tea Party		Declaration of Independence	

Before the Revolution   King George III of England controlled the thirteen colonies under English law and with English soldiers. The colonists paid high taxes on things like tea, stamps, and sugar. When England tried to increase some taxes, the colonists thought it was unfair and became angry. Patrick Henry, a colonial leader, spoke for other colonists when he said, "Give me liberty or give me death!" He wanted the colonies to separate from England.

England sent more soldiers to control the colonies. In 1770, armed British soldiers killed five colonists in the city of Boston. One of the colonial leaders killed was Crispus Attucks, an African-American sailor and escaped slave. This was called the Boston Massacre.

In 1773, the English tried to tax the tea that the colonists drank. Some colonists were angry. They went onto a ship in Boston Harbor and threw 90,000 pounds of tea into the water. This was the Boston Tea Party.

The American Revolution   Most colonists wanted to separate from England. Their taxes were too high. They didn't want British soldiers staying in their homes.

George Washington

13 colonies

They needed to have their own government. They started the Revolutionary War against England in 1775. George Washington was the commander in chief (leader) of the colonial army. The war continued for eight years, until 1783. The colonies won the American Revolution (Revolutionary War). The thirteen colonies became the thirteen original states. Later, George Washington became the first president of the United States. He is called the "Father of Our Country."

Declaration of Independence

Declaration of Independence   In 1776, representatives of the thirteen colonies met at the Second Continental Congress in Philadelphia, Pennsylvania. They discussed independence from England. On July 4, 1776, colonial representatives adopted the Declaration of Independence. The Declaration of Independence announced our independence from Great Britain. Thomas Jefferson was the main writer of the Declaration of Independence. The Declaration said, "All men are created equal." It also said that all people have the right to life, liberty, and the pursuit of happiness. These rights cannot be taken away.

Now, we celebrate July 4th of every year as the Independence Day of the United States.

C. Review the reading. Circle any new words. Add these words to your dictionary. Discuss the new words with your teacher and classmates.

3. After You Read

A. Read the information. Put a ✔ under *True* or *False*. Talk about your answers with your classmates.

1. The English taxed tea, stamps, and sugar.

2. Most colonists were happy with the high English taxes.

3. George Washington was the main writer of the Declaration of Independence.

4. Colonial representatives wrote the Declaration of Independence in 1776.

5. The Declaration of Independence said, "All men are created equal."

6. Two rights in the Declaration of Independence are life and liberty.

	True	False
1.	✔	
2.		
3.		
4.		
5.		
6.		

B. Fill in the blanks with the words below. Read the story with a classmate.

~~taxed~~	1783	Revolutionary War	Declaration of Independence
won	equal	July 4, 1776	tea
free	angry	right	Washington

In 1770, King George III of England controlled the colonies. England

(1) _____taxed_____ the sugar, tea, and stamps of the colonists. English soldiers

guarded the colonies. The colonists were very (2) _____ . Most colonists

wanted to have a (3) _____ and independent country. Some colonists

threw a lot of (4) _____ into Boston Harbor.

The (5) _____ _____ was fought

between England and the American colonists. The war continued from 1775 to

(6) _____ . The Americans (7) _____

the Revolutionary War. The English lost the war. After the war, George (8) _____

became the first president of the United States.

During the war, colonial representatives met and wrote the (9) _____

_____ _____ . The Declaration of Independence

says all men are created (10) _____ . It says people have the

(11) _____ to life, liberty, and the pursuit of happiness. Colonial

representatives adopted it on (12) _____ .

4. Spotlight Readings

The Boston Massacre and the Killing of Crispus Attucks
March 5, 1770

In the 1760s, the British taxed sugar, stamps, and tea. The colonists said, "No taxation without representation!"

The British sent soldiers to Boston, Massachusetts. Some colonists were angry about the soldiers. On March 5, 1770, a small group of between thirty and one hundred Bostonians confronted British soldiers guarding the customs house. The colonists yelled. They carried sticks and clubs. They threw snowballs. The soldiers had guns.

Crispus Attucks was a colonial leader. He was a 47-year-old sailor and fugitive slave. Attucks' father was born in Africa and his mother was Native American.

The British soldiers shot their guns. Crispus Attucks and four other colonists were killed. The people of Boston said Attucks, "... was the first to defy and the first to die." The killings were called the Boston Massacre.

Sybil Ludington *Revolutionary War Heroine*
1761–1839

Sybil Ludington 🏵 *Youthful Heroine*

In April 1777, Danbury, Connecticut was destroyed by British soldiers. Sybil Ludington and her father lived twenty-five miles away, in Patterson, New York. They saw Danbury burning.

After she heard the news about the destruction of Danbury and saw the fire, Sybil rode forty miles on her horse to talk to her neighbors. Sybil organized people to fight the British. She said to meet at her family's house. She said, "The British are burning Danbury. Muster (meet) at Ludington's." After hearing the news, people lit candles in their windows, took out their guns, and got on their horses.

The next morning, four hundred colonists fought the British. British General Tyron, the Governor of New York, and his soldiers were defeated.

Sybil Ludington is an American heroine. In 1777, she was 16 years old. She was congratulated for her heroism by General George Washington.

George Washington *Father of Our Country*
1732–1799

George Washington was an important leader in the history of this country. He led the Continental Army in the American Revolution. Washington was the president of the Constitutional Convention of 1787 that wrote the Constitution. In 1789, Washington was elected by the electoral college as the first president of the United States.

Washington grew up in Virginia. He went to school until age fourteen. He became a surveyor. As the leader of the American Revolution, he was loved by his soldiers and officers.

Washington was a wealthy plantation owner. He had many slaves. He said he did not like slavery, but he did not free his slaves during his lifetime.

Today, George Washington is called the "Father of Our Country." As president, he did not want too much power. He believed citizens should participate in government and take civic responsibility. He did not like corruption.

Thomas Jefferson *Writer of the Declaration of Independence* 1743–1826

Thomas Jefferson was the primary writer of the Declaration of Independence.

Jefferson wrote, "We hold these truths to be self-evident, that all men are created equal." He believed that every citizen was equal and born with the natural rights to life, liberty, and the pursuit of happiness. He said governments cannot take away these rights.

Jefferson also wrote that King George III of England wanted too much money in taxes. The king forced colonists to have soldiers in their homes. Jefferson said the colonies had the right to separate from England.

The Declaration of Independence was adopted on July 4, 1776. Today, the word equality in the Declaration of Independence means that, by law, Americans of all sexes, races, genders, and ethnicities have equal rights to jobs, housing, riding on public transportation, and education.

5. Make It Real

A. Sit in a group of four. Read the scenes below. Talk in your group about one of the scenes.

Scene 1	Scene 2
It is 1773. Imagine you are an English soldier in Boston. Your government is taxing the colonists. You are guarding the colonies for King George III. The colonists are very angry. Talk about how you feel. One group member writes the ideas.	It is 1776. Imagine you are a colonial representative to the Second Continental Congress in Philadelphia, Pennsylvania. You are writing the Declaration of Independence. You think it is necessary to separate from England. Talk about how you feel. One group member writes the ideas.

B. Now, meet a student from another group—either an English solider or a colonial representative. Introduce yourself. Talk about your feelings toward the other group. Talk about the United States. Talk about the future.

6. Real Stories

A. Read a student's story.

About My Life

My name is Mamadou Fall and I was born in Senegal, in western Africa. Many people in Senegal are poor. There is no medical care for them. Most of the children in Senegal don't have money to get vaccinated against diseases. Many children die from malaria.

After I came to the United States in 1997, I went to school to learn English as a Second Language. During that time, I was a security guard at a hospital. Then, I decided to change my career because I wanted to become a nurse. I studied to be a Certified Nursing Assistant (CNA).

Mamadou Fall

Now, I work at one of the best hospitals in the United States. I plan to continue my studies, learn more about medicine, and become a Registered Nurse, an RN, one day. After I become an experienced RN, I would like to travel to Senegal to help the poor and sick children in that country. I want to use what I have learned to help others.

B. Talk to a classmate about these questions:
  1. Where were you born?
  2. When did you come to the United States?
  3. Why did you come to the United States?
  4. What are some things and ideas you brought with you from your country?
  5. What are your future plans?

C. Write a story about your life in the United States.

_____

_____

_____

_____

D. Read your story to a partner. Ask your partner a question about her or his story.

7. Take the Test

This section will give you practice for the Naturalization Test.

CD 1
Track 4

A. Listen to the questions. Circle the correct answers.

1. Who was the main writer of the Declaration of Independence?
   - **a.** George Washington
   - **b.** Thomas Jefferson
   - **c.** Patrick Henry
   - **d.** King George III

2. When was the Declaration of Independence adopted?
   - **a.** January 15, 1770
   - **b.** June 14, 1675
   - **c.** May 31, 1783
   - **d.** July 4, 1776

3. What did the Declaration of Independence say?
   - **a.** The Pilgrims were in America.
   - **b.** The United States was free from Great Britain.
   - **c.** The Boston Tea Party was beginning.
   - **d.** The colonists were happy.

4. What is another name for England?
   - **a.** France
   - **b.** Canada
   - **c.** Mexico
   - **d.** Great Britain

5. Why did the colonists fight the British?
   - **a.** because of high taxes
   - **b.** because the British army stayed in their homes
   - **c.** because they didn't have self-government
   - **d.** all of the above

6. Who said, "Give me liberty or give me death!"?
   - **a.** Thomas Jefferson
   - **b.** George Washington
   - **c.** Patrick Henry
   - **d.** King George III

7. Which president is called the "Father of Our Country"?
   - **a.** Abraham Lincoln
   - **b.** George Washington
   - **c.** John Adams
   - **d.** Alexander Hamilton

8. What is another name for the American Revolution?
   - **a.** Civil War
   - **b.** War of 1812
   - **c.** Revolutionary War
   - **d.** World War I

CD 1
Track 5

B. Now, listen again and check your answers.
Review the questions and answers with your partner. (Answers are at the back of the book on page 157.)

C. Listen to each sentence. Then, listen again and write what you hear.

1. _____

2. _____

3. _____

4. _____

Pairs: Check your partner's answers with the sentences on page 157.

D. N-400 Parts 2 and 3: Information about You and Your Eligibility
Interview a partner. (See pages 106–110 in Unit 10 for additional questions.)

1. What is your Social Security Number?

2. What is your date of birth?

3. When did you become a Lawful Permanent Resident of the United States?

4. Have you ever been absent from the United States since you became a Lawful Permanent Resident?

5. Where were you born?

6. What country are you from?

7. Are you married, single, divorced, widowed, or separated?

E. Clarification: If you don't understand something in the interview, you can say:
Could you please say that again?

8. ★ Think About Your Learning

My favorite activity in this unit was _____ .
I want to study more about

☐ Life in the colonies before the American Revolution

☐ The Revolutionary War

☐ The Declaration of Independence

☐ _____ (other)

9. Game

	What are three rights in the Declaration of Independence? →	What holiday is celebrated on July 4?	Who was the first president of the United States?	★ FINISH ★ ★
When was the Declaration of Independence adopted? ↑	Who was the main writer of the Declaration of Independence?	What is the main idea of the Declaration of Independence?	Who is called the "Father of Our Country"? ←	Which country won the Revolutionary War? ↑
When did the Revolutionary War begin? ↑	Who fought in the Revolutionary War? →		Who was the commander of the U.S. military?	When did the Revolutionary War end?
	Why did the colonists fight in the Revolutionary War?	What happened at the Boston Tea Party?	Who was killed at the Boston Massacre?	Who said, "Give me liberty or give me death!"? ← ↑
★ ★ START ★	Who was the King of England in 1770? →	What are three things the English taxed?	What did the colonists think about taxes?	

Unit 3
The Constitution, the Bill of Rights, and the Amendments

Liberty Bell

Unit Focus

☆ The Constitution of the United States

☆ The Bill of Rights

☆ The Amendments to the Constitution

☆ Spotlight Reading: Benjamin Franklin

Key Vocabulary Preview

Constitutional Convention of 1787	James Madison	checks and balances	Bill of Rights
Constitution	Alexander Hamilton	amendment	freedom of spee
"We the People of the United States … "	market economy (capitalist economy)	the right to bear arms	freedom of relig
Benjamin Franklin	powers of the federal government	vote	freedom of press
Federalist Papers	separation of powers	voting age	freedom of asse

1. **Before You Read**

A. Look at the picture above. Ask your partner these questions.

   1. Who is the leader of your native country—a president, a king or queen, a military leader, or a religious person?

   2. Is the government elected, appointed, or led by the military or a royal family in your native country?

   3. Who makes the laws in your native country?

   4. Did you vote in your native country? Why or why not?

B. Sit in a group of four. Talk about this question. Write your answers in the chart.

   What are some laws of the U.S. government?

   EXAMPLE: You can vote when you are 18 years old.

Laws of the United States

C. Read your answers to the class.

2. Citizenship Reading

A. What do you know about these words? Write your ideas on the lines.

Constitution

Bill of Rights

Amendments

B. Read.

U.S. History: The Law of the Land

Revolutionary War ends		Bill of Rights adopted		Fifteenth Amendment added		Twenty-Sixth Amendment added
1783	**1787**	**1791**	**1865**	**1870**	**1920**	**1971**
	Constitution written		Thirteenth Amendment added		Nineteenth Amendment added	

The Constitution of the United States   After the Revolutionary War, colonial leaders needed to organize a national government. In 1787, they met at the Constitutional Convention in Philadelphia, Pennsylvania. They wanted to protect their rights of freedom, liberty, and equality. They wrote the United States Constitution. Benjamin Franklin was the oldest member at the Constitutional Convention.

The Federalist Papers supported the passage of the U.S. Constitution. Written by Alexander Hamilton, James Madison, and John Jay, the Federalist Papers discussed the ideas in the Constitution. They spread information about the need for a powerful central government.

The Constitution was passed on September 17, 1787, and it was later ratified by the states. The Preamble (introduction) to the Constitution begins with the words, "We the People of the United States."

The Constitution is the plan of government. It defines the government's responsibilities. It is the supreme law of the land. Everyone must follow the law. The federal government can pass laws, collect taxes, print money, organize an army, declare war, and make treaties. Some powers are given to the national government, and some powers are given to the states.

The Constitution establishes a representative democracy (a republic) as our form of government. The economic system in the United States is a market economy. The Constitution guarantees the rights of all people in the United States, both citizens and noncitizens.

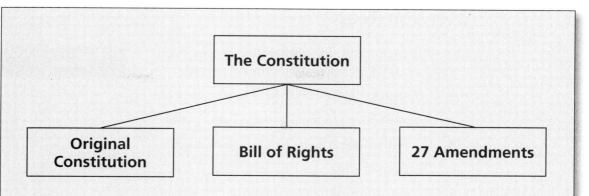

The Constitution
- Original Constitution
- Bill of Rights
- 27 Amendments

There are three branches of government: the executive branch, the legislative branch, and the judicial branch. The separation of powers, called checks and balances, prevents one branch of government from becoming more powerful than the others.

The Bill of Rights   The Constitution can be changed by the people. A change is called an amendment. The first ten amendments are called the Bill of Rights. They were adopted in 1791. The First Amendment guarantees freedom of speech, freedom of the press, freedom of religion, the right to assemble (hold a meeting), and the right to ask for a change of government. Some other amendments in the Bill of Rights guarantee the rights of people accused of crimes. For example, a person accused of a crime has the right to have a lawyer and the right to a trial by jury. The rights of everyone living in the United States, both citizens and noncitizens, include freedom of expression, freedom of speech, freedom of assembly, freedom of worship, freedom to petition the government, and the right to bear arms.

The Amendments to the Constitution   Today, there are twenty-seven amendments to the Constitution. The Thirteenth Amendment freed slaves. It passed in 1865. The Fifteenth Amendment guaranteed former slaves the right to vote. It passed in 1870. The Nineteenth Amendment guaranteed women's right to vote. It passed in 1920. The Twenty-Sixth Amendment to the Constitution established the minimum voting age of 18. It passed in 1971. The right to vote is the most important right of a U.S. citizen. The Fifteenth, Nineteenth, Twenty-Fourth, and Twenty-Sixth Amendments guarantee citizens the right to vote.

C. Review the reading. Circle any new words. Add these words to your dictionary. Discuss the new words with your teacher and classmates.

3. After You Read

A. Read the sentences. Put a ✔ under *True* or *False*. Talk about your answers with your classmates.

	True	False
1.	✔	
2.		
3.		
4.		
5.		
6.		

1. A change to the Constitution is an amendment.
2. There are 30 amendments to the Constitution.
3. The Bill of Rights is the first ten amendments.
4. The Constitution was written in 1787.
5. The Constitution was written in Washington, D.C.
6. The Constitution begins with "We the People of the United States."

B. Fill in the blanks with the words below. Read the story with a classmate.

amendments	Bill of Rights	18	Twenty-Sixth
~~Constitution~~	Philadelphia	vote	twenty-seven
freedom of speech	noncitizens	supreme	government
religion	press	assembly	

The U.S. (1) _____Constitution_____ was written in 1787. The Constitutional

Convention was held in (2) _____ . The Constitution is the

(3) _____ law of the land. It sets up the (4) _____ .

   The (5) _____ _____ _____

is another name for the first ten (6) _____ to the Constitution.

An amendment is a change to the Constitution. Now, there are (7) _____

amendments to the Constitution. The right to (8) _____ is

the most important right guaranteed in the Constitution. A citizen must be

(9) _____ years old to vote. Voting rights are guaranteed in the

Fifteenth, Nineteenth, Twenty-Fourth, and (10) _____ Amendments.

   The Bill of Rights was adopted in 1791. The First Amendment in the Bill of Rights guar-

antees (11) _____ _____ _____ ,

(12) _____ , (13) _____ , and (14) _____ .

The rights of citizens and (15) _____ are guaranteed by the Bill of

Rights and the Constitution.

4. ★ **Spotlight Reading**

Benjamin Franklin
1706–1790

Benjamin Franklin
American diplomat and oldest
member of the Constitutional
Convention

In 1787, fifty-five delegates met to write the United States Constitution. The meeting was in Philadelphia, Pennsylvania. The delegates wanted to protect the rights of freedom, liberty, and equality. At that time, Benjamin Franklin was the oldest member at the Constitutional Convention. He was 81 years old.

Franklin had an interesting life. He was born in Boston, Massachusetts, on January 17, 1706. In his family, there were seventeen children. He loved to read and study, but he could only go to school for two years. Instead, he helped his father make soap and candles to support the family. When he was a young man, Franklin worked for his brother James. James was a printer.

Later, Benjamin Franklin became a printer, a writer, and a publisher. He wrote and published a newspaper. He was the writer of *Poor Richard's Almanac,* which contained weather reports, recipes, and predictions. He was also a scientist and an inventor. He invented a special stove to heat houses, the Franklin stove, and bifocal lenses for glasses. In the 1750s, Franklin experimented with electricity. Franklin started the first free libraries in the United States.

For many years, Franklin lived in Europe. He was a diplomat representing the American colonies. In 1777, he convinced the king of France to send guns, money, and soldiers to America. The money, soldiers, and supplies helped the colonies win the Revolutionary War against England. After returning from France, Franklin freed his slaves.

Franklin died on April 17, 1790. When he died, he was 84. Franklin was one of the Founding Fathers of the United States. Before he died, the colonists won the American Revolution and the U.S. Constitution was written.

5. Make It Real

A. Sit in a group of four. Read the scenes below. Talk in your group about one of the scenes.

Scene 1	Scene 2
It is 1787. It is the time of the Constitutional Convention in Philadelphia. Your group opposes having a single president. You think a president is the same as a king. You are afraid that one rich man will control the new government. Talk about how you feel. One group member writes the ideas.	It is 1787. It is the time of the Constitutional Convention in Philadelphia. Your group favors having an elected president. You think one person can represent all the people. You think a single president will be the best leader. Talk about how you feel. One group member writes the ideas.

B. Now, meet a student from another group. Introduce yourself. Talk about your feelings about having a powerful president. Talk about the United States. Talk about the future.

6. Real Stories

A. Read a student's story.

Coming to the United States

Rovelio Perez

My wife and I came to the United States from Guatemala on foot. We walked for several days. We wanted to have better opportunities for ourselves and for our children. We wanted our children to have a good education. After I arrived, my life was very difficult. I painted cars in body shops for many years. I had to buy all my own masks, uniforms, and equipment. After I came to the United States, my wife left me.

Now, after many years in the United States, I have enough money to support my children. There are more opportunities for jobs. I like the liberty and democracy we have here. In Guatemala, there was a lot of violence and danger. I was afraid to talk about my ideas. In the United States, you can talk about your ideas. You can talk about the government and give your opinion. You can say what you like and what you don't like.

B. Talk to a classmate about freedom of speech.

    ★ What can you talk about in your country? (ideas, government, opinions)

    ★ What can you talk about in the United States? (ideas, government, opinions)

C. Write a story about having freedom of speech in the United States.

_____

_____

_____

_____

_____

_____

D. Read your story to a partner. Ask your partner a question about his or her story.

7. Take the Test

This section will give you practice for the Naturalization Test.

CD 1
Track 7

A. Listen to the questions. Circle the correct answers.

1. What is the supreme law of the United States?
   a. the Constitution
   b. the Declaration of Independence
   c. the Pledge of Allegiance
   d. the "Star-Spangled Banner"

2. What happened at the Constitutional Convention of 1787?
   a. the American Revolution
   b. The Constitution was written.
   c. George Washington became president.
   d. the Boston Tea Party

3. What is the introduction to the Constitution called?
   a. the Bill of Rights
   b. the supreme law of the land
   c. the Preamble
   d. the Declaration of Independence

4. What do we call a change to the Constitution?
   a. a citizen
   b. an amendment
   c. a representative
   d. a report

5. What is one power of the federal government?
   a. to give a driver's license
   b. to print money
   c. to provide police protection
   d. to provide schools

6. Who wrote the Federalist Papers?
   a. Washington and Lincoln
   b. Madison, Hamilton, and Jay
   c. Franklin and Jefferson
   d. Native Americans

7. What is the economic system of the United States?
   a. planned economy
   b. fascism
   c. feudalism
   d. market economy

8. What is one thing Benjamin Franklin is famous for?
   a. He was a soldier in the American Revolution.
   b. He was born in New York.
   c. He started the first free libraries in the United States.
   d. He traveled to Mexico.

CD 1
Track 8

B. Now, listen again and check your answers.
Review the questions and answers with your partner. (Answers are at the back of the book on page 158.)

CD 1
Track 9

C. Listen to each sentence. Then, listen again and write what you hear.

1. _____

2. _____

3. _____

4. _____

Pairs: Check your partner's answers with the sentences on page 158.

D. N-400 Parts 5 and 6A: Your Physical Description and Your Place of Residence
Interview a partner. (See pages 106–110 in Unit 10 for additional questions.)

1. How tall are you?
2. How much do you weigh?
3. What is your race?
4. What color is your hair?
5. What color are your eyes?
6. How long have you lived at your present address?
7. Did you list all the places you've lived in the last five years?

E. Clarification: If you don't understand something in the interview, you can say:
Could you please repeat that?

8. **Think About Your Learning**

My favorite activity in this unit was _____ .
I want to study more about:
☐ The Constitution
☐ The Bill of Rights
☐ The Amendments to the Constitution
☐ _____ (other)

	What is the most important right of U.S. Citizens? →	What is one amendment that guarantees voting rights?	What is the rule of law?	★ FINISH ★ ★
↑				
What are other rights guaranteed by the Bill of Rights?	What is one right guaranteed by the First Amendment?	Whose rights are guaranteed by the Constitution?	Which amendment guaranteed women's right to vote? ←	Which amendment freed the slaves? ↑
What are the three branches of government? ↑	What is one power of the federal government? →		What kind of government does the United States have?	What stops one branch from becoming too powerful?
	How many amendments are there to the Constitution?	What do we call a change to the Constitution?	What are the first three words of the Constitution?	What is the introduction to the Constitution called? ← ↑
★ ★ START ★	What is the supreme law of the land? →	What does the Constitution do?	When was the Constitution written?	

Unit 4
Growth and the Civil War

Abraham Lincoln

African American Slaves

Unit Focus

☆ The United States Grows

☆ Slave or Free?

☆ The Civil War and President Lincoln

☆ Spotlight Reading: Sojourner Truth

Key Vocabulary Preview

lands	Mississippi River	slave	plantations
expand	Missouri River	free	factories
immigrants	Canada	Underground Railroad	assassinated
population	Mexico	the North	Civil War
settlers	north	the Union	Abraham Lincoln
Atlantic Ocean	south	the South	Emancipation
Pacific Ocean	east	Confederacy	Proclamation
Louisiana Purchase	west		Thirteenth Amendment

1. Before You Read

A. Talk about these questions with a partner.

1. Are there political problems or economic problems in your native country?
2. Was there a war there? When?
3. What is or was the reason for the problems?
4. What is or was a way to stop the problems?

B. Sit in a group of four. Find out about your classmates. Fill in the chart.

1. What's your name?
2. Where were you born?
3. Is there a war in your native country?
4. What are your native country's problems?

Name	Country	War	Problems
Isabel	Italy	no	not enough jobs

C. Tell your class about one student in your group.

EXAMPLE: Isabel was born in Italy. There is no war now. The people need more jobs.

2. Citizenship Reading

A. What do you know about these words? Write your ideas on the lines.

Slavery   Freedom

B. Read.

U.S. History: Expansion and the Civil War

		Emancipation Proclamation issued		Lincoln assassinated	
United States expands territory					
1800–1853	**July, 1861**	**January 1, 1863**	**April 9, 1865**	**April 14, 1865**	**1865**
	Civil War begins		Civil War ends		Thirteenth Amendment adopted

The United States Grows   In 1775, there were thirteen colonies in the United States. Between 1800 and 1853, the country expanded west to the Pacific Ocean. In 1803, the United States bought the Louisiana Territory from France. With the Louisiana Purchase, the lands of the United States expanded west across the Mississippi and the Missouri Rivers. These two rivers are the longest rivers in the United States.

The United States acquired lands from England, France, Spain, and Mexico. All of these lands originally belonged to the Native Americans (American Indians.) By 1853, the United States stretched from the Atlantic Ocean in the east to the Pacific Ocean in the west. Canada was to the north. Mexico was to the south.

The population increased. Many people moved to the southern and western parts of the United States. After 1840, many new immigrants came from Europe and Asia. They wanted freedom, land, and better jobs. The U.S. government forced the Native Americans off their own lands and gave the lands to settlers.

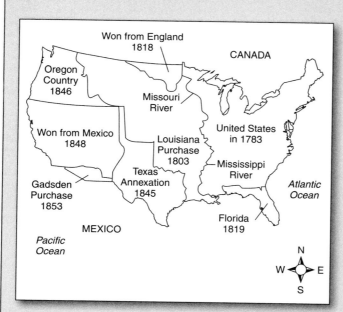

Slave or Free? From the 1600s to the 1800s, people from different areas of Africa were forced to come to the United States as slaves. They were brought by slave traders. In Africa, they were free. They were bought and sold in the United States. Many worked on Southern plantations (large farms). Some escaped to freedom in the North on the Underground Railroad. The Underground Railroad was organized by people opposed to slavery.

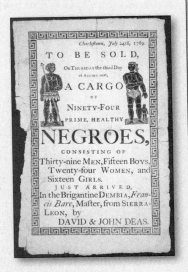

Separate cultures developed in the North and the South. Most white Southerners believed in slavery. Nearly one-third of all white southerners owned black slaves. The economy of the South depended on farming cotton and slavery. The people in the South believed in the rights of the individual states and in a small federal government. The economy of the North depended on industry and the growth of cities. Factory workers in the North made shoes, clothing, guns, and tools. Many people in the North were against the expansion of slavery into new states and territories.

The Civil War and President Lincoln The northern and southern states were divided on the issue of slavery. Between 1861 and 1865, the North (the Union) and the South (the Confederacy) fought the Civil War. The Civil War began after the South seceded (separated) from the Union. More than 600,000 soldiers died in the Civil War.

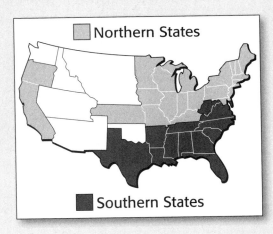

Abraham Lincoln was elected the sixteenth president in 1860. Lincoln was president during the Civil War. He wanted to keep the North and the South together as one nation. He did not want the Union to be divided. On January 1, 1863, Lincoln signed the Emancipation Proclamation. The Emancipation Proclamation freed the slaves in the Confederate states.

On April 9, 1865, the North won the Civil War. The Thirteenth Amendment was passed in 1865. It ended slavery. Lincoln was assassinated on April 14, 1865. Americans remember Lincoln because he united the country and freed slaves. His birthday, February 12, is a national holiday.

C. Review the reading. Circle any new words. Add these words to your dictionary. Discuss the new words with your teacher and classmates.

3. After You Read

A. Look at the map on page 35. Fill in the answers.

1. What ocean is to the east of the United States? _____
2. What country is north of the United States? _____
3. Name one of the two longest rivers in the United States. _____
4. What country is south of the United States? _____
5. What ocean is to the west of the United States? _____
6. What country is north of Mexico? _____

B. Fill in the blanks with the words below. Read and compare your sentences with a classmate.

1. a. The American Revolution began in 1778.
   b. The Civil War began in _____ .
2. a. In the Revolutionary War, the colonists fought against the English.
   b. In the Civil War, the North (Union) fought against the _____ .
3. a. George Washington was the president after the American Revolution.
   b. _____ _____ was the president during the Civil War.
4. a. Colonial representatives signed the Declaration of Independence.
   b. Abraham Lincoln signed the _____ _____ .

C. Fill in the blanks with the words below. Read the story with a classmate.

slaves	~~expanded~~	free	Mississippi River	Louisiana
North	South	immigrants	Africa	slavery
won	Civil	Thirteenth	Emancipation Proclamation	

Between 1800 and 1853, the United States (1) _____expanded_____ west to

the Pacific Ocean. The United States bought the (2) _____

Territory from France in 1803. Settlers crossed the (3) _____

_____ and the Missouri River

as they moved west. After 1840, many new

(4) _____ came from countries

in Europe and Asia.

People from (5) _____ were

brought to the United States by slave traders. African

(6) _____ worked on plantations in the

South. The slaves were not (7) _____ .

Frederick Douglass
African-American anti-slavery leader

The states in the (8) _____ wanted workers to be free. The states in

the (9) _____ wanted to have slaves. The Civil War was fought over

(10) _____ .

   The (11) _____ War was fought between 1861 and 1865.

Abraham Lincoln was the president. The North (12) _____ the war.

In 1863, Lincoln signed the (13) _____ _____ .

It freed the slaves. In 1865, the (14) _____ Amendment ended slavery.

4. Spotlight Reading

Sojourner Truth
1787–1883

Sojourner Truth was an African slave born in 1797 in New York State. Her original name was Isabella. She was one of thirteen children, but she did not know all her brothers and sisters. She and some of her brothers and sisters were sold as slaves.

Isabella was a tall, strong woman who worked as a house slave. In her young life, she was physically and sexually abused by slave masters. She had five different masters. She could not read or write. She was illiterate. Inspired by conversations with God, she escaped to freedom.

In her lifetime, Sojourner Truth became a preacher, an abolitionist, and a supporter of women's rights. She opposed slavery. She told other people about the experiences of slaves. *The Narrative of Sojourner Truth* was written about her life as a slave.

Sojourner Truth, a northern slave who was freed. She fought for the rights of slaves and all men and women.

Sojourner Truth worked to include black soldiers in the Union (Northern) Army during the Civil War. In 1864, Abraham Lincoln honored her at the White House. After the Civil War, she fought to give land to slaves who were freed.

Sojourner Truth was a feminist who supported women's rights and women's suffrage (women having the right to vote). It is reported that Sojourner Truth gave her famous speech "Ain't I a Woman?" in 1851. She said men and women should be treated equally. "I could work as much and eat as much as a man—and bear the lash as well! And ain't I a woman?" She said she "plowed and reaped and husked and chopped and mowed. Can any man," she asked, "do more than that?"

Sojourner Truth died in 1883. She was an important fighter against slavery and for the rights of all men and women.

5. Make It Real

A. Sit in a group of four. Read the scenes below. Talk in your group about one of the scenes.

Scene 1	Scene 2
It is 1850. You are an African slave forced to come to America. You live on a Southern plantation. You want to escape to the North. Talk to the other slaves about why you want to be free. One group member writes the ideas.	It is 1850. You are a Southern plantation owner. You are a religious person. You own 100 slaves. You say God thinks slavery is good for African people. Talk to other plantation owners about how you feel. One group member writes the ideas.

B. Now, meet a student from another group—an African slave or a Southern plantation owner. Introduce yourself. Talk about your feelings toward the other group. Talk about your past. Talk about slavery. Talk about the plantation. Talk about the future.

6. Real Stories

A. Read a student's story.

Leaving My Native Country

In December 1988, there was a very strong earthquake of 6.9 near my hometown, Kirovakan, Armenia. Many beautiful stone buildings in our town collapsed. Many children were killed. More than 25,000 people died. My good friend died along with one of her children. Many new cemeteries were built in my country after the earthquake.

Gohar Baghdasaryan

The earthquake came in December. At that time, it was very cold. Many people were homeless. People lived anywhere they could. Some survivors moved to live with friends and family, some lived in school buildings. Some families moved to other Soviet republics, some to the United States. My family moved to Yerevan, Armenia, to live with my mother-in-law. In that city, the economy was very bad. Factories were closed. I could not find another job as an economist.

Years later, I applied to come to the United States. I was lucky—I won the lottery! My husband and I came here in 2005. I am happy to be here, but my son still lives in Armenia. We try to visit him as often as we can.

B. Talk to a classmate about these questions:

1. How long did you live in your native country?
2. What were the political or economic problems in your native country?
3. Why did you leave your country?
4. Who did you leave behind when you came here?

C. Write a story about why you left your native country and who you left behind.

_____

_____

_____

_____

_____

_____

_____

D. Read your story to a partner. Ask your partner a question about his or her story.

7. Take the Test

This section will give you practice for the Naturalization Test.

**CD 1
Track 10**

A. Listen to the questions. Circle the correct answers.

1. What lands did the United States buy in 1803?

   a. Oregon Territory   **c.** Louisiana Territory
   b. Texas   **d.** Gadsden Purchase

2. Name one of the two longest rivers in the United States.

   a. Mississippi River   **c.** Columbia River
   b. Colorado River   **d.** Snake River

3. Name the U.S. war between the North and the South.

   a. American Revolution   **c.** Civil War
   b. War of 1812   **d.** French and Indian War

4. Name one problem that led to the Civil War.

   a. expansionism   **c.** international relations
   b. slavery   **d.** geography

5. What group of people was taken to America and sold as slaves?

   a. Pilgrims   **c.** British
   b. colonists   **d.** Africans

6. What did the Emancipation Proclamation do?

   a. gave women the vote   **c.** ended the Civil War
   b. gave freedom of speech **d.** freed the slaves in the
                                      Confederate states

7. Which president freed the slaves?

   a. Abraham Lincoln   **c.** John Adams
   b. Thomas Jefferson   **d.** George Washington

8. What is another name for the Civil War?

   a. Korean War   **c.** World War I
   b. Vietnam War   **d.** the War between the North
                                      and the South

B. Now, listen again and check your answers.
Review the questions and answers with your partner. (Answers are at the back of the book on page 160.)

C. Listen to each sentence. Then, listen again and write what you hear.

1. _____

2. _____

3. _____

4. _____

5. _____

Pairs: Check your partner's answers with the sentences on page 160.

D. N-400 Parts 6B and 7: Your Employment and Travel (See pages 106–110 in Unit 10 for additional questions.)

1. Where do you work now?

2. Where have you worked in the last five years?

3. Are you a student? Where do you go to school?

4. How many days were you out of the United States in the last five years?

5. How many trips of 24 hours or more have you taken outside of the United States in the last five years? Where did you go?

E. Clarification: If you don't understand something in the interview, you can say:
Could you say that again please?

8. Think About Your Learning

My favorite activity in this unit was _____ .
I want to study more about:

- ☐ Growth and Expansion
- ☐ Abraham Lincoln
- ☐ the Civil War
- ☐ Slavery
- ☐ The Emancipation Proclamation
- ☐ _____ (other)

9. ★ Game

	The _____ Amendment ended slavery.	Sojourner Truth fought for the _____ of slaves and all men and women.	Frederick Douglass spoke against _____ .	★ FINISH ★ ★
	Lincoln was _____ in 1865.	The Civil War ended in _____ .	Over _____ soldiers died in the Civil War.	The Emancipation Proclamation _____ the slaves.
The _____ Railroad freed some slaves.	Lincoln was the _____ during the Civil War.		The Civil War began in _____ .	Lincoln issued the _____ in 1863.
The _____ fought against the South in the Civil War.	Most people in the North wanted workers to be _____ .	Southern plantation owners wanted _____ to farm the land.	_____ were slaves on Southern plantations.	_____ were brought to America by slave traders.
★ ★ START ★	After 1800, the United States expanded _____ to the Pacific Ocean.	The United States bought _____ from France in 1803.	After 1840, many new _____ came from Europe and Asia.	The Mississippi and the _____ are the longest rivers in the United States.

Unit 5
Twentieth and Twenty-First Centuries

Women Factory Workers during WW II

Dr. Martin Luther King, Jr.

Unit Focus

☆ Industrialization and Labor

☆ Women's Suffrage

☆ World War I (1914–1918)

☆ The Great Depression and the New Deal

☆ World War II (1939–1945)

☆ The United Nations

☆ The Cold War and the Vietnam War

☆ Dr. Martin Luther King, Jr. and Civil Rights

☆ Terrorist Attack (September 11, 2001)

☆ Spotlight Reading: Susan B. Anthony

Key Vocabulary Preview

factory workers	Great Depression	United Nations	Susan B. Anthony
women's suffrage	New Deal	Cold War	Elizabeth Cady Stanton
discrimination	World War II	Vietnam War	Woodrow Wilson
World War I	Soviet Union	Civil Rights movement	Franklin Delano Roosevelt
Allies	bomb	terrorist attack	Dwight D. Eisenhower
enemy	atomic bomb		Dr. Martin Luther King, Jr.

1. Before You Read

A. Sit in a group of four. Make a list of things about the United States that are different from your native country.

more cars	taller buildings	

B. What are some things about your life now that are different from your life in your native country? Fill in the chart.

	Native Country	United States
1. Time you get up?		
2. Clothes you wear?		
3. Food you eat?		
4. People you live with?		
5. Your job?		
6. Hours you work?		
7. Time you spend with friends and family?		

C. Talk about this question with your partner.
Is your life easier or more difficult in the United States? Why?

EXAMPLE: My life is more difficult because I work longer hours.

2. Citizenship Reading

A. What do you know about these words? Write your ideas on the lines.

The Depression

World War II

Civil Rights

B. Read.

U.S. History: From Industrialization into the Twenty-First Century

World War I	Great Depression begins		World War II		Vietnam War Era		Cold War	
1914– 1918	**1920**	**1929**	**1932**	**1939– 1945**	**1946**	**1961– 1973**	**1963**	**1947– 1990**	**Sept. 11, 2001**
	Nineteenth Amendment adopted	New Deal		First meeting of the United Nations		Dr. Martin Luther King, Jr. speech "I Have a Dream"		Terrorists attack U.S.

Industrialization and Labor Factories and machinery were developed in the United States beginning in the mid-1820s. Many people left farms and moved to cities to find jobs. Immigrants came from other countries to live in cities and work in factories. By the 1920s, more than 50 percent of the U.S. population lived in cities.

Factory workers' lives were difficult in the early 1900s. They worked ten to twelve hours a day for very low pay. For the first time, their working day was controlled by a time clock. Children worked in factories. Working conditions were not safe. Some factory owners discriminated against immigrants, nonwhites, and women.

Women workers protest unfair labor practices.

Workers fought for and won shorter work days, rest periods, better pay, and safer jobs. Some workers organized into labor unions. The U.S. Congress passed laws restricting child labor.

Women's Suffrage In this same period, women's organizations led by Susan B. Anthony, Elizabeth Cady Stanton, and other women's leaders fought for and won the right for women to vote (women's suffrage). This right became law when the Nineteenth Amendment passed in 1920.

World War I   World War I, or the Great War, began in 1914. Woodrow Wilson was the president. The United States tried to stay out of the war. It did not want to be involved in the problems of other countries. In 1917, after Germany bombed U.S. ships, the United States entered the war. England, France, Russia, and the United States were the Allies. The Central Powers: Germany, Austria-Hungary, and Turkey were the enemy. The war was fought over land, power, and money. World War I ended in 1918. The war helped the United States become a world power.

Franklin Delano Roosevelt

The Great Depression and the New Deal
In the 1930s, the United States had many economic problems. Businesses and banks were forced to close. People lost their jobs and their savings. Many people lost their homes, had no money, and were hungry. People organized and demanded help from the government.

Franklin Delano Roosevelt was president from 1932 to 1945, during the Great Depression and World War II. His plan to rebuild the country was called the New Deal. The New Deal created new jobs. People built roads, dams, post offices, and theaters. The government helped some small businesses to get loans. Roosevelt wanted to keep the economy going. Congress passed the Social Security Act and welfare programs. The minimum wage was established for some workers.

World War II   World War II began in 1939. After the Japanese bombed Pearl Harbor on December 7, 1941, the United States entered the war. England, France, Russia, and the United States were the Allies, as in World War I. Dwight D. Eisenhower was general of the army during World War II. The Axis Powers of Germany, Italy, and Japan were the enemy. Hitler, the dictator of Germany, wanted to control all of Europe. More than ten million Jews, Catholics, homosexuals, and gypsies were killed by Hitler and the Nazis during the Holocaust.

In August 1945, the United States dropped atomic bombs on the Japanese cities of Hiroshima and Nagasaki. The war ended in August 1945. The Allies won World War II.

The United Nations   After World War II, world leaders came together to form the United Nations. They wanted to avoid further conflict. The United Nations (UN) met for the first time in 1946. In the UN, representatives from countries discuss and try to resolve world problems. The UN also gives economic aid to many countries for medical and educational needs.

The Cold War and the Vietnam War   The United States and Russia were allies in World War II. After the war, the United States had a strong economy and powerful weapons. The Russians (the Soviet Union, the Soviets) lost more than twenty million people during the war, but they had a very large military. Both countries were superpowers.

The Soviets wanted to control Eastern Europe. They wanted to spread Communism in Eastern Europe and throughout the world. The United States wanted to stop the spread of Communism. The conflict between the United States and the Soviet Union was called the Cold War. The Cold War was a war of words and military power. It was never a war with actual fighting. In the 1970s, the Soviet Union and the United States built nuclear weapons for protection. The Cold War continued from the middle of the 1940s until the early 1990s when the Soviet Union collapsed.

U.S. soldiers fought in the Vietnam War. The United States sent troops to Vietnam in 1961. Many Americans opposed the war because they didn't think the United States had a good reason to be in Vietnam. Many other Americans supported the war. Finally, in 1973, a peace treaty was signed. Most U.S. soldiers left Vietnam in 1973.

Dr. Martin Luther King, Jr. and Civil Rights

Since the time of slavery, African Americans have fought for civil rights and equal treatment. One Civil Rights movement leader was Dr. Martin Luther King, Jr. In his famous speech "I Have a Dream," he said, "I have a dream that my four little children will one day live in a nation where they will not be judged by the color of their skin, but by the content of their character." He was assassinated in 1968. Dr. Martin Luther King, Jr.'s birthday is a national holiday and is celebrated on the third Monday in January.

Dr. Martin Luther King, Jr.

Asian Americans, Latinos, Native Americans, and people of other nationalities have fought for their civil rights. Women, gays (homosexuals), senior citizens, and disabled groups have fought against discrimination. The fight for equality continues to this day.

Terrorist Attack   On September 11, 2001, terrorists attacked the United States. They hijacked four planes and destroyed the twin towers of the World Trade Center in New York City. They crashed a plane into the Pentagon. Another plane crashed in Pennsylvania. Over 3,000 people died.

C. Review the reading. Circle any new words. Add these words to your dictionary. Discuss the new words with your teacher and classmates.

3. After You Read

A. Read the sentences. Put a check ✔ under *True* or *False*.

1. Woodrow Wilson was President during World War I.
2. In the Depression, most people had a lot of food and money.
3. In World War II, Germany wanted to control Europe.
4. In 1945, the United States dropped bombs on Japan.
5. The Vietnam War was before World War II.
6. Dr. Martin Luther King, Jr. fought for the civil rights of all Americans.
7. During the Cold War, the United States wanted to stop Communism.

	True	False
1.	✔	
2.		
3.		
4.		
5.		
6.		
7.		

B. Fill in the blanks with the words below. Read the story with a classmate.

speech	bombs	Dr. Martin Luther King, Jr.	world problems
Russia	1939	Franklin Delano Roosevelt	terrorists
1918	~~shorter~~	England	Communism

In the early 1900s, workers fought for (1) _____ shorter _____ work

days, better pay, and better working conditions. The United States was an ally of

(2) _____ , France, and (3) _____ in

World War I. World War I ended in (4) _____ . After World War I,

the United States was a world power.

(5) _____ _____ _____

was president during the 1930s and the Great Depression. World War II began in

(6) _____ . In 1945, the United States dropped two atomic

(7) _____ on Japan. After World War II ended, the United Nations

met in 1946 to discuss (8) _____ _____ .

(9) _____ _____ _____

_____ _____ was a famous Civil Rights leader.

He gave his (10) _____ "I Have a Dream" in 1963.

During the Cold War, the United States wanted to stop (11) _____ .

On September 11, 2001, (12) _____ attacked the United States.

More than three thousand people died.

4. Spotlight Reading

Susan B. Anthony
1820–1906
Women's Suffrage Leader

Elizabeth Cady Stanton and
Susan B. Anthony

Susan B. Anthony was born in 1820 in Massachusetts. She was the daughter of a Quaker factory owner and reformer. In her lifetime, Susan was a teacher, a reformer, and a women's rights activist.

Susan B. Anthony's first experience of discrimination was as a teacher in 1846. She discovered a male teacher was making $10 a month, but she was getting only $2.50 for the same work.

In July 1848, the first women's right convention met in Seneca Falls, New York. One of its leaders was Elizabeth Cady Stanton. The Declaration of Rights and Sentiments was passed. It demanded women have the same rights as men. It demanded women have the right to vote.

In 1851, Susan B. Anthony met Elizabeth Cady Stanton. Both women believed that the idea that men were superior to women was false. They believed that women should own property and be able to vote. Susan B. Anthony organized many women's meetings and conventions. She talked about women's equality. Stanton was the writer; Anthony was the organizer.

During the Civil War, Anthony and Stanton organized the Women's Loyal National League to guarantee the freedom of African Americans. After the Civil War ended, Stanton and Anthony worked for universal suffrage (voting rights for all women and men, both blacks and white). In 1869, they founded the National Woman Suffrage Association. They wanted women to have equality with men and the right to vote.

The Nineteenth Amendment passed in 1920. Because of the work of Anthony and Stanton and many other women's leaders, over eight million American women voted for the first time in history on November 2, 1920.

5. Make It Real

A. Sit in a group of four. Read the scenes below. Talk in your group about one of the scenes.

Scene 1	Scene 2
You are a factory worker. You work ten to twelve hours a day. Your boss refuses to pay you for working overtime. Talk about how you feel. One group member writes the ideas.	You work for the U.S. Department of Labor. Your job is to make sure workers are paid for overtime work. Talk to the other government workers. What can you do to help the factory worker? One group member writes the ideas.

B. Now, meet a student from another group—either a factory worker or someone who works for the U.S. Department of Labor. Introduce yourself. Talk about employee's rights and responsibilities. Talk about employer's rights and responsibilities.

6. Real Stories

A. Read a student's story.

Finding a Better Life

In Egypt, the country where I was born, life is very hard. A lot of people don't have jobs. It is not easy to find work. When I was young, I was trained as a carpenter. My father, uncles, and cousins are all carpenters. It is our family tradition. We make furniture and cabinets. We work with our hands and with machines.

When I was young, I trained with my uncle. After working with my uncle, I left Egypt and moved to Jordan to find work. Later on, I moved to Iraq. Each time I moved, I was looking for a better job.

I came to the United States with my family because I was looking for a better life. I wanted to find a good job. Finding work here is easier. The United States helps people find jobs. People here are very friendly and helpful. Now, my life is good, much better than my life in Egypt.

Salah Marzok

B. Read the story again. Talk to a classmate about this question:
How has Salah's life changed since he came to the United States?

C. Think about Salah's story. Then, look back at the questions on page 45. Write a story about changes in your life.

_____

_____

_____

_____

_____

_____

_____

D. Read your story to a partner. Ask your partner a question about his or her story.

7. Take the Test

This section will give you practice for the Naturalization Test.

CD 1
Track 13

A. Listen to the questions. Circle the correct answers.

1. What did Susan B. Anthony do?
   - **a.** She fought in World War II.
   - **b.** She was a soldier in the American Revolution.
   - **c.** She fought for women's rights.
   - **d.** She freed the slaves.

2. Which countries were our enemies during World War II?
   - **a.** England, France, and Russia
   - **b.** China, Japan, and Korea
   - **c.** England, Spain, and Portugal
   - **d.** Germany, Japan, and Italy

3. What was the main concern of the United States during the Cold War?
   - **a.** fascism
   - **b.** Communism
   - **c.** capitalism
   - **d.** terrorism

4. Who was Dr. Martin Luther King, Jr.?
   - **a.** a scientist
   - **b.** a Civil Rights leader
   - **c.** a famous musician
   - **d.** president of the United States

5. What movement tried to end racial discrimination?
   - **a.** the Civil Rights movement
   - **b.** the Welfare Rights movement
   - **c.** the Cold War
   - **d.** the Great Depression

6. Name one war fought by the United States in the 1900s.
   - **a.** the American Revolution
   - **b.** the Civil War
   - **c.** the War of 1812
   - **d.** World War I

7. Who was president during World War I?
   - **a.** Woodrow Wilson
   - **b.** Dwight D. Eisenhower
   - **c.** Franklin Roosevelt
   - **d.** Abraham Lincoln

8. What event happened in the United States on September 11, 2001?
   - **a.** Japan attacked the United States.
   - **b.** Terrorists attacked the United States.
   - **c.** World War I began.
   - **d.** United Nations began.

CD 1
Track 14

B. Now, listen again and check your answers.
Review the questions and answers with your partner. (Answers are at the back of the book on page 161.)

C. Listen to each sentence. Then, listen again and write what you hear.

1. _____

2. _____

3. _____

4. _____

Pairs: Check your partner's answers with the sentences on page 161.

D. **N-400 Part 8: Your Marital History** Interview your partner. (See pages 106–110 in Unit 10 for additional questions.)

1. Are you married?

2. How many times have you been married?

3. What is your present spouse's full name?

4. When were you married?

5. Where was your spouse born?

6. Is your spouse a citizen?

7. When did your spouse become a citizen?

E. Clarification: If you don't understand something in the interview, you can say:
Could you please say that again more slowly?

8. Think About Your Learning

My favorite activity in this unit was _____ .

I want to study more about:

☐ World War I

☐ World War II

☐ The United Nations

☐ The Cold War and the Vietnam War

☐ Civil Rights

☐ _____ (other)

9. Game

	What did Dr. Martin Luther King, Jr. do? →	What movement tried to end racial discrimination?	What happened on September 11, 2001?	FINISH
When did the Vietnam War end? ↑	What does the United Nations (UN) do?	What happened in the Holocaust?	Who won World War II?	Who were the Axis Powers in World War II?
Name three programs that were part of the New Deal. ↑	When did World War II begin? →		Name a general in World War II.	Who were the Allies in World War II? ↑
Who was the president during the Great Depression and World War II?	Name three things that happened in the Great Depression.	Who were the Allies in World War I?	In what year did World War I end?	Why did the United States want to stay out of World War I? ↑
START	Name four things workers fought for and won in the early 1900s. →	What did Susan B. Anthony do?	In what year did World War I begin?	Who was president during World War I?

Unit 6
Celebrations and Symbols

The Statue of Liberty in New York Harbor

Unit Focus

☆ The United States Flag

☆ "The Star-Spangled Banner"

☆ The Pledge of Allegiance

☆ United States Holidays

☆ Spotlight Reading:
   The Statue of Liberty

Key Vocabulary Preview

United States Flag	"The Star-Spangled Banner"	New Year's Day	Labor Day
stars	national anthem	Martin Luther King, Jr. Day	Columbus Day
stripes	Pledge of Allegiance	Presidents' Day	Veterans Day
Alaska	loyal	Memorial Day	Thanksgiving Day
Hawaii	liberty	Flag Day	Christmas Day
national symbol	justice	Independence Day	
Statue of Liberty	holidays		

1. Before You Read

A. Sit in a group of four. Look at the pictures above. Talk about the questions.

1. When are Flag Day and Independence Day celebrated in the United States?
2. What are some things people do on those days?
3. Are Flag Day and Independence Day celebrated in your native country?
4. What are some things people do?

B. Find out about your classmates. Fill in the chart.

1. What is your name?
2. What country are you from?
3. What are the colors of your country's flag?
4. What symbols are in your country's flag?

   What other symbols represent your country?

Name	Country	Flag Colors	Symbols
Arturo	Mexico	red, white, green	eagle

C. Tell your class about one student in your group.

EXAMPLE: Arturo is from Mexico. His country's flag is red, white, and green. The eagle is a symbol of his country.

2. Citizenship Reading

A. What do you know about these words? Write your ideas on the lines.

```
_____
_____    ( The United      _____    ( The Pledge of
_____      States Flag )    _____      Allegiance )
```

```
_____
_____    ( United States
_____      Holidays )
```

B. Read.

CD 2
Track 19

> ### Holidays and Symbols of the United States
>
> **The United States Flag**   The 13 stripes in the United States flag represent the original 13 colonies. The 50 white stars represent the 50 states of the United States. The colors of the United States flag are red, white, and blue. The stripes in the flag are red and white. The red means courage, the white means purity. The blue in the flag represents justice. Alaska was the 49th state and Hawaii was the 50th state.
>
> Flag Day is celebrated on June 14. On this day, many people put a flag in front of their homes, schools, and businesses.
>
> **"The Star-Spangled Banner"**
> "The Star-Spangled Banner" is the national anthem, or song, of the United States. Francis Scott Key wrote the words in 1814. At that time, British soldiers told Francis Scott Key they were going to destroy Fort McHenry and the American flag flying over the fort. They said he would never see that flag again. The next morning, the Americans were victorious and Francis Scott Key saw the flag was still flying. He wrote the words to the song.
>
> The United States Congress declared "The Star-Spangled Banner" the national anthem
>
> > **The Star-Spangled Banner**
> >
> > Oh, say can you see,
> >   By the dawn's early light,
> > What so proudly we hailed
> >   At the twilight's last gleaming,
> > Whose broad stripes and bright stars,
> >   Through the perilous fight,
> > O'er the ramparts we watched
> >   Were so gallantly streaming?
> > And the rockets' red glare,
> >   The bombs bursting in air,
> > Gave proof through the night
> >   That our flag was still there.
> > O, say, does that
> >   Star-Spangled Banner yet wave
> > O'er the land of the free
> >   And the home of the brave?

The Pledge of Allegiance

I pledge allegiance
to the Flag
of the United States of America,
and to the Republic
for which it stands,
one Nation
under God,
indivisible,
with Liberty
and Justice for all.

in 1931. People sing "The Star-Spangled Banner" on holidays and at some public ceremonies. Stand and face the flag when you sing "The Star-Spangled Banner."

CD 2
Track 20

The Pledge of Allegiance   The Pledge of Allegiance is a promise by citizens to be loyal to the government of the United States and to give up loyalty to other countries. Citizens promise to defend the Constitution and obey U.S. laws. The Pledge of Allegiance says that the 50 states make up one nation that is indivisible (it cannot be divided). The Pledge of Allegiance says that, in the United States, there is liberty (freedom) and justice (fairness) for all people. When you say The Pledge of Allegiance, stand and face the flag. Put your right hand over your heart.

United States Holidays   Holidays are celebrated throughout the year in the United States. New Year's Day is celebrated on January 1, the first day of the year. Dr. Martin Luther King, Jr.'s birthday is a national holiday we celebrate on the third Monday in January. He was a famous Civil Rights leader. We celebrate Presidents' Day on the third Monday in February. On that day, President Washington's and President Lincoln's birthdays are remembered. Memorial Day is observed on the last Monday in May. On Memorial Day, we remember the men and women who died in military service to the United States.

On July 4, people in the United States celebrate Independence Day. On that day, we remember when the Continental Congress declared independence from England (Great Britain). Labor Day, the first Monday in September, honors working people. Columbus Day, on October 12, celebrates the arrival of Christopher Columbus in the Americas. Veterans Day is celebrated on November 11. On that day, we remember U.S. veterans who have served in all wars. On the fourth Thursday in November, we celebrate Thanksgiving. After their first harvest in 1621, the Pilgrims celebrated Thanksgiving with the Native Americans (American Indians). Christmas is celebrated on December 25. On that day, Christians celebrate the birth of Jesus Christ. Other Americans celebrate December 25 as a nonreligious holiday. Schools, banks, post offices, and government offices are closed on Christmas. Most stores are also closed. Other religious groups celebrate holidays at this time of year, such as Hanukkah and Kwanzaa.

National Holiday	Date Celebrated	Purpose
New Year's Day	January 1	begins the new year
Martin Luther King, Jr. Day	third Monday in January	commemorates the Civil Rights leader
Presidents' Day	third Monday in February	honors President Washington and President Lincoln
Memorial Day	last Monday in May	honors men and women in military service
Independence Day	July 4	celebrates independence from England (Great Britain)
Labor Day	first Monday in September	honors working people
Columbus Day	October 12	commemorates Columbus's arrival in the Americas
Veterans Day	November 11	honors all U.S. veterans
Thanksgiving	fourth Thursday in November	celebrates the first Thanksgiving
Christmas	December 25	celebrates the birth of Jesus Christ (Other religious holidays celebrated during this time of year include Hanukkah and Kwanzaa.)

C. Review the reading. Circle any new words. Add these words to your dictionary. Discuss the new words with your teacher and classmates.

3. After You Read

A. Read the sentences. Put a ✔ under *True* or *False*.

1. At the first Thanksgiving, Pilgrims celebrated with Native Americans.
2. Presidents' Day is in June.
3. Memorial Day honors men and women who died in the military.
4. Independence Day is on July 4.
5. Labor Day is in November.
6. New Year's is a month-long celebration.

	True	False
1.	✔	
2.		
3.		
4.		
5.		
6.		

B. Read the sentences. Put a ✔ in the correct column. You may check more than one column.

1. You put your hand over your heart.
2. Francis Scott Key wrote the words in 1814.
3. You sing, "Oh, say can you see…"
4. "One Nation under God, indivisible, with liberty and justice for all."
5. You promise to be loyal to the United States. You give up loyalty to other countries.
6. You stand up.

	The Pledge of Allegiance	"The Star-Spangled Banner"
1.	✔	
2.		
3.		
4.		
5.		
6.		

C. Match the information.

_____ **1.** The 13 stripes in the flag represent

_____ **2.** The 50 stars in the flag represent

_____ **3.** "The Star-Spangled Banner" is

_____ **4.** July 4 is

a. the 50 states.

b. the national anthem.

c. Independence Day.

d. the 13 original colonies.

D. Fill in the blanks with words below. Read the story with a classmate.

republic	~~stripes~~	Pledge	The Star-Spangled Banner
colonies	states	anthem	Independence Day
justice	stars	Statue	

The American flag is red, white, and blue. It has 13 (1) _____stripes_____

and 50 (2) _____ . The red and white stripes represent the original 13

(3) _____ . The white stars are for the 50 (4) _____

of the United States. (5) _____ _____

_____ _____ is the name of our national song.

Francis Scott Key wrote the national (6) _____ in 1814. July 4 is

(7) _____ _____ .

The (8) _____ of Allegiance says we are one nation. "I pledge

allegiance to the flag of the United States of America, and to the (9) _____

for which it stands, one nation, under God, indivisible, with liberty and (10) _____

for all."

The (11) _____ of Liberty is in New York Harbor on Liberty Island.

4. Spotlight Reading

The Statue of Liberty

The Statue of Liberty is a national symbol of liberty and freedom for people around the world. The Statue of Liberty is located in New York Harbor on Liberty Island.

In her right hand, the Statue of Liberty holds a torch. The torch represents enlightenment. On her head, she wears a crown. The rays in the crown represent the seven seas and the seven continents of the world. The Statue of Liberty is 112 feet high. The statue is made from copper. Because of weathering, the copper color is light green.

The people of France gave the Statue of Liberty to the people of the United States. Frédéric-Auguste Bartholdi, a French sculptor, designed the statue.

Celebrations and Symbols

It was officially dedicated in 1886. The statue celebrates the friendship between the United States and France.

At the feet of the Statue of Liberty is the poem "The New Colossus" written by Emma Lazarus, a Jewish American. The poem expresses the feelings of new immigrants who come to the United States.

The New Colossus (1883)

Not like the brazen giant of Greek fame,
With conquering limbs astride from land to land;
Here at our sea-washed, sunset gates shall stand
A mighty woman with a torch, whose flame
Is the imprisoned lightning, and her name
Mother of Exiles. From her beacon-hand
Glows world-wide welcome; her mild eyes command
The air-bridged harbor that twin cities frame.
"Keep ancient lands, your storied pomp!" cries she
With silent lips. "Give me your tired, your poor,
Your huddled masses yearning to breathe free,
The wretched refuse of your teeming shore.
Send these, the homeless, tempest-tost to me,
I lift my lamp beside the golden door!"

5. Make It Real

A. Sit in a group of four. Read the scenes below. Talk in your group about one of the scenes.

Scene 1	Scene 2
Imagine you are Francis Scott Key. One night you are watching a battle of the War of 1812. When you wake up the next morning, the American flag is still flying. You feel very proud. Talk about how you feel. One group member writes the ideas.	Imagine you are becoming a citizen of the United States. It is almost 200 years after Francis Scott Key wrote the "Star-Spangled Banner." You are going to sing the song at your naturalization (citizenship) ceremony. Talk about how you feel. One group member writes the ideas.

B. Now, meet a student from another group—either Francis Scott Key or a new citizen of the United States. Introduce yourself. Talk about the United States. Talk about its past and its future. Talk about how things have changed.

6. Real Stories

A. Read a student's story.

How I Feel When I Look at the Flag

Elian Sayegh

When I look at the flag of the United States, I have very strong feelings. The flag of the United States is very unique. I like the red, white, and blue colors of the flag. People from all over the world know and like these colors. The U.S. flag is different from the flags of other countries. It has stars and stripes. When I look at the flag, it gives me a lot of positive energy.

Before, I lived in Syria. Now, I am living in the United States. In the United States, the system works very well. The laws here apply to everyone, to the rich and to the poor. Most people have jobs, clothing, and enough food to eat. Everyone here has to pay his or her taxes. Here, life is very good.

B. Talk to a classmate about these questions:

1. Before you came to the United States, how did you feel when you looked at the U.S. flag?
2. How do you feel now when you look at the flag?

C. Write a story about the U.S. flag. You can write about how you feel when you see it, what it symbolizes to you, or any experience you have had with the American flag.

_____

_____

_____

_____

_____

_____

D. Read your story to a partner. Ask your partner a question about her or his story.

7. Take the Test

This section will give you practice for the Naturalization Test.

CD 1
Track 16

A. Listen to the questions. Circle the correct answers.

1. What do we show loyalty to when we say The Pledge of Allegiance?
   - **a.** Great Britain
   - **b.** the United States
   - **c.** France
   - **d.** the Statue of Liberty

2. Why does the flag have 13 stripes?
   - **a.** because there were 20 original colonies
   - **b.** because there were 13 original colonies
   - **c.** because of Alaska and Hawaii
   - **d.** to represent the 50 states

3. Why does the flag have 50 stars?
   - **a.** one for each state in the country
   - **b.** one for each of the 13 colonies
   - **c.** "The Star-Spangled Banner"
   - **d.** the Pledge of Allegiance

4. What is the name of the national anthem?
   - **a.** The Statue of Liberty
   - **b.** "The Star-Spangled Banner"
   - **c.** The Pledge of Allegiance
   - **d.** Independence Day

5. When do we celebrate Independence Day?
   - **a.** July 4
   - **b.** May 31
   - **c.** June 14
   - **d.** December 25

6. Name two national U.S. holidays.
   - **a.** Bill of Rights and Constitution Day
   - **b.** Easter Sunday and Election Day
   - **c.** Memorial Day and Labor Day
   - **d.** Mother's Day and Father's Day

7. What do we celebrate on Veterans Day?
   - **a.** We honor all U.S. veterans.
   - **b.** We celebrate our independence.
   - **c.** We remember the first Thanksgiving.
   - **d.** We begin a new year.

8. On which holiday do we honor working people?
   - **a.** Presidents' Day
   - **b.** Christmas Day
   - **c.** Memorial Day
   - **d.** Labor Day

B. Now, listen and check your answers.
Review the questions and answers with your partner. (Answers are at the back of the book on page 163.)

C. Listen to each sentence. Then, listen again and write what you hear.

1. _____

2. _____

3. _____

4. _____

5. _____

Pairs: Check your partner's answers with the sentences on page 163.

D. N-400 Parts 9A and B and 10A: Your Children and Other Questions Interview your partner. (See pages 106–110 in Unit 10 for additional questions.)

1. How many children have you had?
2. What are their names, birth dates, places of birth, and current addresses?
3. Have you ever claimed to be a U.S. citizen in writing or any other way?
4. Have you ever registered to vote in any Federal, state, or local election in the United States?
5. Have you ever voted in any Federal, state, or local election in the United States?
6. Since becoming a Lawful Permanent Resident, have you ever failed to file a required federal, state, or local tax return?
7. Do you owe any federal, state, or local taxes that are overdue?
8. Have you ever been declared legally incompetent or been confined to a mental institution within the last five years?

E. Clarification: If you don't understand something in the interview, you can say:
Could you please say that again more slowly?

8. Think About Your Learning

My favorite activity in this unit was _____ .

I want to study more about:

❏ The Pledge of Allegiance
❏ "The Star-Spangled Banner"
❏ The United States Flag
❏ United States Holidays
❏ _____ (other)

	Say the Pledge of Allegiance. →	When do we sing "The Star-Spangled Banner"?	Name the forty-ninth and fiftieth states.	★ FINISH ★ ★
↑	When you say the Pledge of Allegiance, put your right hand over your _____ .	Name two national U.S. holidays.	What poem is written at the base of the Statue of Liberty?	Where is the Statue of Liberty? ← ↑
What day is Veterans Day?	What is the name of the national anthem? →		Who wrote the song "The Star-Spangled Banner"?	What does the Statue of Liberty represent?
↑	What day is Presidents' Day?	On what day is Dr. Martin Luther King, Jr.'s birthday celebrated?	What day is Independence Day?	What are the three colors in the flag? ← ↑
★ ★ START ★	How many stars are in the flag? →	Why does the flag have fifty stars?	Why does the flag have thirteen stripes?	

Unit 7
The Legislature

Dome of the U.S. Capitol Building

Unit Focus

☆ The Federal Government and Congress

☆ The Legislative Branch

☆ The Senate

☆ The House of Representatives

☆ Powers of Congress

☆ Elections

☆ Spotlight Reading: The U.S. Capitol Building

Key Vocabulary Preview

federal government	Capitol Building	election	citizen
Congress	Senate	elected	law
legislative branch	senators	re-elected	veto
judicial branch	House of Representatives	political parties	candidate
executive branch	representatives		separation of powers
Washington, D.C.	Speaker of the House		checks and balances

1. Before You Read

A. Discuss the question below. Write your answer.

What are the rules in our class?

EXAMPLE: Arrive on time.

Turn off cell phones in class.

_____

_____

_____

_____

B. Work with a partner. Ask your partner these questions:

1. What are the rules in this school?

2. Who makes the rules in our school?

3. Do you think more rules are needed?

4. How do adult students participate in making the rules at this school?

C. Work with your partner. Write two new rules for your school or for your class.

EXAMPLE: Keep the school clean.

_____

_____

_____

_____

D. Read your ideas to the class.

2. Citizenship Reading

A. What do you know about these words? Write your ideas on the lines.

the House of Representatives

the Senate

B. Read.

U.S. Government: The Legislature

The Federal Government and Congress   There are three branches of the U.S. government: the legislative branch, the judicial branch, and the executive branch. All three branches of the U.S. government meet in Washington, D.C. Washington, D.C. is the capital of the United States.

The Legislative Branch   The legislative branch is the Congress. Congress makes the federal laws. There are two parts of Congress, the House of Representatives and the Senate. Congress meets at the Capitol Building in Washington, D.C. All the members of the House of Representatives and Senate are elected by the people. Citizens vote for the U.S. senators and representatives from their state. U.S. senators and representatives represent all the people from their state.

Nancy Pelosi, Speaker of the House of Representatives

The Senate   There are 100 senators in the Senate. Each state has two senators. Each senator is elected for a six-year term. A senator must be at least 30 years old and a U.S. citizen. Senators can be re-elected. The leader of the Senate is the vice president of the United States.

The House of Representatives
There are 435 voting members of the House of Representatives. The number of representatives a state has depends on how many people live in that state. A state with a large population has more representatives. A state with a small population has fewer representatives.

Each representative is elected for a two-year term. Representatives must be at least 25 years old and a U.S. citizen. They can be re-elected. The leader of the House of Representatives is called the Speaker of the House.

The Legislature

Powers of Congress   Congress has the power to declare war, make laws, collect taxes, borrow money, control immigration, and set up a judicial system and postal system. To become a law, a bill must pass in the House of Representatives and Senate. Then, the president signs the bill into law. If the president vetoes (rejects) the bill, the bill goes back to the Senate and the House to be voted on again. It must pass in the Senate and the House with a two-thirds majority vote. Then, the bill becomes a law.

The separation of powers, called checks and balances, prevents one branch of government (the legislative branch, the judicial branch, or the executive branch) from becoming more powerful than the others.

Elections   Candidates representing political parties can run for federal office (president, vice president, representative and U.S. senator) on Election Day. The two major political parties in the United States are the Democratic Party and the Republican Party. Independent parties such as the Green Party also run and elect candidates to political office. To vote in an election, a citizen must be at least 18 years old.

C. Review the reading. Circle any new words. Add these words to your dictionary. Discuss the new words with your teacher and classmates.

3. After You Read

A. Study the chart. Ask your partner four questions about the chart.

The Legislative Branch = The Congress		
	Senate	**House of Representatives**
How many?	100 senators	435 representatives
How long?	6-year term	2-year term
Age?	30 years old	25 years old
Leader?	vice president	Speaker of the House

B. Read the sentences. Put a check ✔ in the correct column. You may check more than one column.

1. There are 435 elected members.
2. The elected term is for six years.
3. It is a part of Congress.
4. Bills are passed there.
5. The leader is the vice president.

	House of Representatives	Senate
1.	✔	
2.		
3.		
4.		
5.		

C. Fill in the blanks with the words below. Read the story with a classmate.

laws	~~Congress~~	vice president	18
Senate	president	435	Democratic
100	House of Representatives	Speaker	Republican

(1) _____Congress_____ is the legislative branch of the U.S. government.

Congress makes the federal (2) _____ . The (3) _____

and the (4) _____ _____ _____

are the two parts of Congress. After a bill passes the House and the Senate, the

(5) _____ must sign it.

There are (6) _____ senators in the U.S. Senate. The leader of the Senate is the (7) _____ _____ . There are (8) _____ voting members in the House of Representatives. The leader of the House is the (9) _____ of the House. Senators and representatives can be re-elected.

To vote in an election, a citizen must be at least (10) _____ years old. The two major political parties in the United States are the (11) _____ and (12) _____ parties.

4. Spotlight Reading

The U.S. Capitol Building

The Capitol Building is located in Washington, D.C., on Capitol Hill. It houses the legislative branch of government. Both the U.S. Senate and the House of Representatives (the Congress) meet in the Capitol Building. In the Capitol Building, members of Congress write, debate, and pass bills that can become federal laws. (After the president approves and signs a bill, it becomes a federal law.)

The Capitol was constructed between the years 1793 and 1824. It has a central dome above two wings (sides). President George Washington laid the cornerstone of the building in 1793. Several different architects designed the building. Both slaves and free workers constructed the Capitol Building. From 1793 until it was completed, the Capitol was constructed, burnt, extended, and restored. A new dome was finished in 1863.

The building has two wings, the House Wing and the Senate Wing. The building contains 540 rooms. On the top of the iron dome of the Capitol is the bronze Statue of Freedom. This statue was created by American sculptor Thomas Crawford. The Statue of Freedom is nineteen feet, six inches tall.

On the inside walls of the Capitol are murals of the great moments in the history of the United States. Some of the murals were painted by Italian-American artist Constantino Brumidi, beginning in 1856.

5. Make It Real

A. Talk about these questions with your teacher and your classmates:

1. The U.S. senators from this state are _____ and _____ .

2. The U.S. representatives from this area are _____ and _____ .

3. The Speaker of the House of Representatives is _____ .

U.S. Representative, John Conyers, Jr.

B. Sit in a group of four. Read the scenes below. Talk in your group about one of the scenes.

Scene 1	Scene 2
Imagine you are a U.S. senator or representative. There is a problem of violence in your area. You are writing a bill to control who can have or use a gun. Talk to the people from your group about how you feel. One group member writes the ideas.	Imagine you are a community member. You are at a neighborhood meeting. There are gang problems in your neighborhood and problems with guns. You think every person must protect herself or himself. Talk about how you feel. One group member writes the ideas.

C. Now, meet a student from another group—either a member of Congress or a community member. Introduce yourself. Talk about neighborhood problems. Talk about a solution.

6. Real Stories

A. Read a student's story.

A New Country, A New Language

When I arrived in the United States, I couldn't speak English. I was afraid to talk to people. I was afraid to go to the market. If I wanted to buy something at the store, I didn't know how to explain what I wanted. I had to take my husband with me to the market. If I went shopping alone, I brought coupons with me and pointed at the pictures. When my neighbors said hello, I didn't know what to say.

Sarah Ping Hu

My first English teacher was so friendly and nice. He understood what I was saying! I loved him because I could talk to him in English. Now, I am taking a citizenship class at an adult school. I feel comfortable speaking English. My neighbors, friends, classmates, and coworkers understand me. Everyone is so friendly in the United States.

B. Talk to a classmate about these questions:

1. When you arrived in the United States, did you speak English?
2. Who was the first person you could communicate with in English?
3. How do you feel when you are speaking English now?

C. Write a story about your experiences speaking English.

_____

_____

_____

_____

_____

_____

D. Read your story to a partner. Ask your partner a question about his or her story.

7. **Take the Test**

This section will give you practice for the Naturalization Test.

CD 1
Track 19

A. Listen to the questions. Circle the correct answers.

1. What is the legislative branch of government?
   - **a.** the president
   - **b.** the vice president
   - **c.** Congress
   - **d.** the judiciary

2. What are the two parts of the U.S. Congress?
   - **a.** the Senate
     and the House of Representatives
   - **b.** the judicial and executive branches
   - **c.** the Capitol Building
     and the Treasury Building
   - **d.** Washington Monument
     and Lincoln Memorial

3. How many U.S. senators are there?
   - **a.** 50
   - **b.** 100
   - **c.** 200
   - **d.** 435

4. The House of Representatives has how many voting members?
   - **a.** 50
   - **b.** 100
   - **c.** 200
   - **d.** 435

5. Why do some states have more representatives than other states?
   - **a.** because they have more land
   - **b.** because they have more people
   - **c.** because they have more money
   - **d.** because they have more water

6. Who makes federal laws?
   - **a.** political parties
   - **b.** the judiciary
   - **c.** Congress
   - **d.** the president

7. What stops one branch of government from becoming too powerful?
   - **a.** political parties
   - **b.** representatives
   - **c.** Congress
   - **d.** checks and balances

8. Who vetoes bills?
   - **a.** the judiciary
   - **b.** the president
   - **c.** Congress
   - **d.** political parties

CD 1
Track 20

B. Now, listen again and check your answers.
Review the questions and answers with your partner. (Answers are at the back of the book on page 164.)

The Legislature

C. Listen to each sentence. Then, listen again and write what you hear.

1. _____

2. _____

3. _____

4. _____

5. _____

6. _____

Pairs: Check your partner's answers with the sentences on page 164.

D. N-400 Part 10B: Affiliations Interview your partner. (See pages 106–110 in Unit 10 for additional questions.)

1. Have you ever been a member of or associated with any organization, fund, foundation, club, or similar group in the United States or in any other place?

2. Have you ever been a member of or in any way associated with: the Communist Party? A totalitarian party? A terrorist organization?

3. Have you ever advocated the overthrow of any government by force or violence?

4. Have you ever persecuted any person because of race, religion, national origin, or membership in a particular social group or political opinion?

5. Between March 23, 1933, and May 8, 1945, did you work for or associate in any way with the Nazi government of Germany or any of its affiliates?

E. Clarification: If you don't understand something in the interview, you can say:
I'm sorry. Do you mean _____ *or* _____ ?

8. Think About Your Learning

My favorite activity in this unit was _____ .

I want to study more about:

☐ The Legislative Branch

☐ The Senate

☐ The House of Representatives

☐ Elections

☐ _____ (other)

9. **Game**

What are the three branches of government?	What is the minimum voting age?	Who is one of your state's U.S. senators?	Name your U.S. representative.	**FINISH**
What are four things Congress can do?	Can a senator or representative be re-elected?	Who is the leader of the House of Representatives?	Who is the leader of the Senate?	Why do some states have more representatives than other states?
Who does a U.S. senator represent?	The House of Representatives has how many voting members?		How old must a representative be?	How long is one term in the House of Representatives?
How old must a senator be?	How long is one term in the Senate?	Why are there 100 senators?	How many senators are there?	How are senators and representatives chosen?
START	What is the legislative branch of government called?	What are the two parts of Congress?	Where does Congress meet?	What does Congress do?

Unit 8
The Executive and Judicial Branches

The Supreme Court Building

Unit Focus

☆ The Executive Branch

☆ The President and the Vice President

☆ The Cabinet

☆ The Judicial Branch

☆ Spotlight Reading: The White House

Key Vocabulary Preview

president	enforce the laws	vote	judicial branch
vice president	commander in chief of the military	electoral college	Supreme Court
White House	term of office	Election Day	chief justice of the Supreme Court
cabinet	inaugurate	Inauguration Day	justices
executive branch		natural-born citizen	

Barack Obama, Forty-fourth President of the United States

A. Sit in a group of four. Look at the picture above. Talk about the questions. Write your answers in your book.

1. Who is the president of the United States? _____

2. What does the president do? _____

3. Who is the vice president of the United States? _____

4. What does the vice president do? _____

5. What other people advise the president? _____

6. What is the Supreme Court? _____

7. What does the Supreme Court do? _____

8. Who is the chief justice of the Supreme Court? _____

9. What is the political party of the president now? _____

B. Read your answers to your class.

2. Citizenship Reading

A. What do you know about these words? Write your ideas on the lines.

the Executive Branch

the Judicial Branch

B. Read.

U.S. Government: The Executive and Judicial Branches

The Executive Branch   The executive branch enforces the laws passed by Congress. The president, vice president, and the Cabinet are the executive branch. The president is in charge of the executive branch.

The Department of Homeland Security (DHS), the Central Intelligence Agency (CIA), the Federal Bureau of Investigation (FBI), the U.S. Citizenship and Immigration Service (USCIS), the Environmental Protection Agency (EPA), and the U.S. Postal Service (USPS) are some of the agencies in the executive branch.

The President and the Vice President   The president is the leader of the country. The president is also the leader of the executive branch. The president signs bills into law, enforces the law, prepares budgets, and is the commander in chief of the military. The president may also veto bills. The president lives and works in the White House. The address of the White House is 1600 Pennsylvania Avenue NW, Washington, D.C. The vice president helps the president and is the leader of the Senate.

The president and the vice president are each elected for a term of four years and can serve for two terms. We vote for the president and vice president on Election Day. It is the first Tuesday after the first Monday in November. In January, the president and vice president are inaugurated (sworn into office).

General Information   To be president or vice president, a person must be a natural-born citizen of the United States, must be at least 35 years old, and must have lived in the United States for fourteen years. If the president can no longer serve, the vice president becomes the president. If the both the president and the vice president can no longer serve, the Speaker of the House becomes the president. The president and vice president

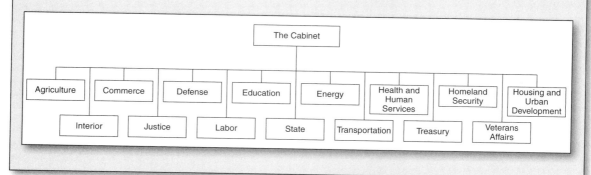

are not directly elected by the people. The people vote for the members of the electoral college. The electoral college members vote for the president and vice president.

The Cabinet   The cabinet advises the president. There are fifteen cabinet members. The cabinet is appointed by the president. Some cabinet members are the Secretary of State, the Secretary of Defense, the Secretary of Homeland Security, the Secretary of Commerce, the Secretary of Housing and Urban Development, the Secretary of Labor, and the Secretary of Education.

The Judicial Branch   The judicial branch of the U.S. government includes the Supreme Court and the federal courts. The courts review and interpret (explain) the laws that the legislative branch makes. The Supreme Court is the highest court in the United States. There are nine justices (judges) on the Supreme Court.

The nine justices are appointed by the president and ratified (approved) by Congress. The chief justice is the leader of the Supreme Court. The justices listen to the cases brought by the people. They decide the cases based on the Constitution and the laws of the United States. Supreme Court decisions are final.

C. Review the reading. Circle any new words. Add these words to your dictionary. Discuss the new words with your teacher and classmates.

3. After You Read

A. Study the chart. Ask your partner the questions below.

The President and the Vice President	
How long?	Four-year term
Age?	At least 35 years old
Birth?	Born a citizen of the United States
Terms?	Can be re-elected to a second term

B. Read the questions. Put a check ✔ in the correct column.

	The Executive Branch (the president)	The Judicial Branch (the justices)
1. Who lives and works in the White House?	✔	
2. Who interprets the Constitution and the laws?		
3. Who enforces the laws?		
4. Who is appointed by the president?		
5. Which branch is led by the chief justice?		

C. Fill in the blanks with the words below. Read the story with a classmate.

electoral college	~~executive~~	four	terms
cabinet	November	vice president	Supreme Court
president	explains	nine	Speaker

The leader of the (1) _____executive_____ branch is the (2) _____ .

The president is elected for (3) _____ years. The president can serve for

two (4) _____ . Election Day is in (5) _____ .

Inauguration Day is in January.

The (6) _____ _____ elects the president.

The (7) _____ advises the president. If the president can no longer

serve, the (8) _____ _____ becomes president.

If the president and vice president can no longer serve, the (9) _____ of the House becomes president.

The (10) _____ _____ is the highest court in the United States. The Supreme Court reviews and (11) _____ the Constitution and the laws. There are (12) _____ justices on the Supreme Court.

4. Spotlight Reading

The White House

The White House

The White House is the official home and workplace of the president of the United States. It is located at 1600 Pennsylvania Avenue NW, in Washington, D.C.

The White House was first completed in 1800. After it was burned by the British in 1814, the White House was rebuilt. John Adams, the second president of the United States, was the first president to live in the White House. Every president, except George Washington, has lived in the White House.

The White House has six floors and 132 rooms. The "first family," the president's family, lives on two of the floors. The East Room, the Green Room, the Blue Room, the Red Room, and the State Dining Room are the most famous rooms. The president and first lady use these rooms to entertain guests and meet leaders from other countries.

The president's office is the Oval Office. In the Oval Office, the president signs bills and executive orders. He meets with staff, visitors, and guests in the Oval Office.

5. Make It Real

A. Sit in a group of four. Read the scenes below. Talk in your group about one of the scenes.

Scene 1	Scene 2
Imagine you are one of a group of senior citizens, over 65 years old. The people in your group are receiving money from social security, but it is not enough money to live on. Talk to the other people about how you feel. One group member writes the ideas.	Imagine you are the president. There are many problems in your country: education, poverty, health care, and jobs. You want to help senior citizens live good lives, but there isn't sufficient money in the budget to give them more. Talk to your cabinet. One group member writes the ideas.

B. Now, meet a student from another group—either a senior citizen or the president. Introduce yourself. Talk about the problems of getting older. Talk about federal budget problems.

6. Real Stories

A. Read a student's story.

The Educational System

I prefer the educational system in the United States to the one in South Korea. Here in this country, students can express their own ideas. My son has gone to school in the United States for the last few years. He likes to speak in front of people and never hesitates to give his opinion. In Korea, students are not accustomed to answering questions in class because they are raised to be humble. In Korea, students never contradict their teacher's ideas.

American students study actively. They go to the library and search the Internet for information. Even elementary school students like to do research and interview people to gather information. In Korea, students don't know how to study independently. They just learn to memorize the answers to questions before taking a test.

Jin Kee

B. Talk to a classmate about these questions:

    1. What are some things you like about the educational system of the United States?

    2. What are some things you'd like to see improved in the educational system?

C. Write your opinion about the educational system.

_____

_____

_____

_____

_____

_____

_____

D. Read your story to a partner. Ask your partner a question about her or his story.

7. Take the Test

This section will give you practice for the Naturalization Test.

CD 2
Track 1

A. Listen to the questions. Circle the correct answers.

1. What is the executive branch of our government?
   - **a.** the president, vice president, cabinet, and departments
   - **b.** the Capitol Building
   - **c.** the Senate and the House of Representatives
   - **d.** the Supreme Court

2. Who is in charge of the executive branch?
   - **a.** the vice president
   - **b.** the cabinet
   - **c.** the president
   - **d.** the chief justice of the Supreme Court

3. What are two cabinet-level positions? (Circle two answers.)
   - **a.** Secretary of Agriculture
   - **b.** Secretary of Land Management
   - **c.** Secretary of Labor
   - **d.** Secretary of War

4. How many Supreme Court justices are there?
   - **a.** six
   - **b.** twelve
   - **c.** three
   - **d.** nine

5. What does the judicial branch do?
   - **a.** reviews and explains the laws
   - **b.** declares war
   - **c.** makes the laws
   - **d.** amends the Constitution

6. In what month do we vote for president?
   - **a.** October
   - **b.** November
   - **c.** December
   - **d.** January

7. What is the highest court in the United States?
   - **a.** municipal court
   - **b.** state court
   - **c.** the Supreme Court
   - **d.** traffic court

8. Where does the president live and work?
   - **a.** the White House
   - **b.** the Capitol Building
   - **c.** the Supreme Court
   - **d.** the Treasury Building

CD 2
Track 2

B. Now, listen again and check your answers.
Review the questions and answers with your partner. (Answers are at the back of the book on page 166.)

C. Listen to each sentence. Then, listen again and write what you hear.

1. _____

2. _____

3. _____

4. _____

Pairs: Check your partner's answers with the sentences on page 166.

D. N-400 Parts 10C and 10D: Your Residency and Your Moral Character Interview your partner. (See pages 106–110 in Unit 10 for additional questions.)

1. Since becoming a Lawful Permanent Resident of the United States, have you ever called yourself a "nonresident" on a Federal, state, or local tax return?

2. Have you ever failed to file a Federal, state, or local tax return because you considered yourself to be a "nonresident"?

3. Have you ever committed a crime or offense for which you were not arrested?

4. Have you ever been arrested, cited, or detained by any law enforcement officer (including USCIS or military officers) for any reason?

5. Have you ever been charged with committing any crime or offense?

6. Have you ever been convicted of a crime or offense?

E. Clarification: If you don't understand something in the interview, you can say: *I'm sorry. I don't understand your question.*

8. Think About Your Learning

My favorite activity in this unit was _____ .

I want to study more about:

❏ The President

❏ The Cabinet

❏ The Vice President

❏ The Supreme Court

❏ _____ (other)

 **Game**

	How many Supreme Court justices are there? →	How are the justices selected?	Who is the chief justice of the Supreme Court?	FINISH ★ ★ ★
↑ What is the highest court in the United States?	What are two cabinet-level positions?	How many terms can a president serve?	What is the address of the White House?	What is the name of the president now? ← ↑
Who signs bills into law?	Who can veto bills? →		What does the president's cabinet do?	If the president can no longer serve, who becomes president?
↑ How long is the president's term?	Name three requirements to be president.	In what month do we vote for president?	Who is in charge of the executive branch?	Which branch enforces the laws? ← ↑
START ★ ★ ★	How many branches of government are there? →	Name the three branches of government.	Which branch of government passes the laws?	Which branch reviews and explains the laws?

Unit 9
State and Local Government

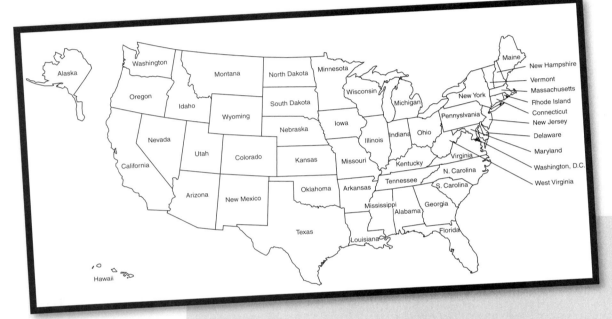

The United States

Unit Focus

☆ State Geography and History

☆ State Government

☆ Local Government: Towns, Cities, and Counties

☆ Spotlight Reading: Rosa Parks

Key Vocabulary Preview

state	mayor	state flower	public protection	fire
capital	city council	state bird	public safety	parks
governor	city commission	education	jails	trash pick up
state senators	county board of supervisors	welfare	libraries	public transportation
state representatives	county commission	roads	schools	health care
state laws	city manager		police	

1. Before You Read

A. Talk about these questions with your teacher and your classmates. Fill in your answers.

State Geography and History	
1. What is the name of this state?	
2. Is this state in the northern, southern, eastern, western, or middle part of the United States?	
3. What is the capital of this state?	
State Government	
4. Who is the governor of this state?	
5. What are the legislative branches of this state?	
6. Who are the state senators or representatives from this area?	
7. What is the highest court in this state?	
Local Government	
8. Who is the mayor (chief executive) of this city?	
9. Is there a city council or city commission?	
10. Is there a county board of supervisors or county commission?	
11. Is there a city manager?	

B. Find out some other information about this state: the population, the year this state joined the Union, the state flower, and the state bird. Share the information with your class.

2. Citizenship Reading

A. What do you know about these words? Write your ideas on the lines.

```
_____                                          _____
                    ( governor )    ( mayor )
_____                                          _____
```

B. Read.

U.S. Government: State and Local Government		
State Government		
Executive Branch	**Legislative Branch**	**Judicial Branch**
Governor	State Senators and State Representatives	State Supreme Court and lower State Courts

State Government   Each of the 50 states has its own government and constitution. Like the federal government, each state government has three branches: the legislative, the executive, and the judicial. The chief executive of the state is the governor. The governor enforces state laws. The state legislature makes the state laws. State laws must agree with the U.S. Constitution. States make laws about work, school, property, and marriage. State senators, state representatives, and state government officials are elected by the people. States raise money from taxes. States provide services in schooling and education, public protection (police) and safety (fire), jails, welfare, roads, public health, and regulation of businesses.

Local Government		
Executive Branch	**Legislative Branch**	**Judicial Branch**
Mayor or City Manager	City Council or County Commission	Municipal Court and Superior Court

Local Government: Towns, Cities, and Counties   The local governments in each area are different. The chief of your local government may be the mayor or the city manager. A city council or city commission may make the laws for your city. A county board of supervisors or county commission may make the laws for your county. City and county governments provide public services. Libraries, schools, police, fire, trash pick up, parks, public transportation, and health care are some of the services provided.

C. Review the reading. Circle any new words. Add these words to your dictionary. Discuss the new words with your teacher and classmates.

3. After You Read

A. Read the questions. Put a check ✔ in the correct column. You may check more than one column.

1. The chief executive is the president.
2. The chief executive is the governor.
3. There are three branches of government: legislative, executive, and judicial.
4. The Constitution is the highest law.
5. The capital is in Washington, D.C.

	Federal	State
1.	✔	
2.		
3.		
4.		
5.		

B. Fill in the blanks with the words below OR with the names of local and state government officials. Read the story with a classmate.

judicial	mayor	legislative	education
~~constitution~~	governor	libraries	public protection
city council	trash		

There are 50 states in the United States. Each state has a (1) _____constitution_____ .

Each state government has three branches, the (2) _____ , the

executive, and the (3) _____ branches. The chief executive of each state

is the (4) _____ .

The governor of our state is (5)_____ . The capital of

our state is (6) _____ . Some services that states provide are

(7) _____ and (8) _____ _____ .

The chief executive of a local government may be the (9) _____ .

The mayor of our city is (10) _____ . In some cities, a

(11) _____ _____ makes the laws for the

residents. Some services provided by cities are (12) _____ pick up and

(13) _____ .

Rosa Parks
Mother of the Civil Rights Movement
1913–2005

Rosa Parks was born in Tuskegee, Alabama, in 1913. She grew up on a small farm with her mother, brother, and grandparents. Rosa attended a one-room school that only went up to the sixth grade. As a child, she was afraid the Ku Klux Klan (KKK) would burn down her house.

In 1955, city buses in Montgomery, Alabama, were segregated. Segregation meant that African Americans could not sit in the same bus seats as whites. African Americans had to give up their seats for white people.

On December 1, 1955, Rosa was living in Montgomery, Alabama. At that time, she was working as a seamstress. Rosa and her husband, Raymond, worked for the National Association for the Advancement of Colored People (NAACP). Rosa got on a bus to go home from work. She sat down in the middle of the bus because there were no seats in the "colored section" at the back. African Americans were allowed to sit in the middle section only if there were no white people who wanted to sit down. The bus continued and more white people got on. They needed to sit down. The bus driver told all the African Americans in Rosa's row to get up and move to the back of the bus where they could stand. They all moved, except Rosa. Rosa refused to move from her seat. She didn't want to be treated as a second-class citizen.

When Rosa didn't move, the bus driver stopped the bus. He got a policeman. The policeman arrested her for violating the segregation law and took her to jail. African Americans in Alabama decided to boycott (not use) city buses to protest her arrest. Dr. Martin Luther King, Jr. was the leader of the bus boycott.

Rosa's case against the state of Alabama went all the way to the U.S. Supreme Court. On November 13, 1956, the Supreme Court ruled that segregation on buses was unconstitutional (not legal). Rosa's refusal to stand up on the bus and give up her seat helped stop segregation in the South!

To celebrate the victory, the next day Rosa and Dr. Martin Luther King, Jr. got on a city bus in Montgomery, Alabama, and sat down right at the front of the bus. In 1997, President Bill Clinton awarded Rosa the Medal of Freedom in recognition of her work for civil rights.

5. Make It Real

A. Sit in a group of four. Read the scenes below. Talk in your group about one of the scenes.

Scene 1	Scene 2
Imagine you are a citizen. In your community, there are many poor, working people who do not have enough money for medical care. The public health clinics need more tax dollars to stay open. Go to a public meeting. Give your opinion about why you think more tax money must be used for public health programs.	Imagine you are a state senator. The economy of your state is bad. Your state has lost a lot of tax money. Talk to the other senators on your health care committee. How can you find extra money to keep public health programs open?

B. Now, meet a student from another group—either a citizen in the community or a state senator. Introduce yourself. Talk about why all people need good public health care. Talk about tuberculosis, AIDS, and other illnesses. What can you do?

6. Real Stories

A. Read a student's story.

Memories of War

While I was a teenager growing up in Iran, there was an eight-year war with Iraq. I was only 13 years old when the war started. The war disrupted my life.

Two of my cousins were killed in that war. They were soldiers. My brother was also a soldier in the war with Iraq. Because of the war, I had to become an adult when I was only a child. Children of my generation didn't have the opportunity to enjoy being teenagers. Those times of war were very hard for my family.

After I moved to the United States, my sister and I attended a 4th of July event on Independence Day. When I heard the firecrackers explode, it reminded me of the war. The noise of the firecrackers sounded like the missiles Iraq shot at Iran.

There is a heaviness in my heart when I think about war. I don't want people to be killed. I want there to be peace in the whole world.

Mahdokht Habibian

B. Talk to a classmate about this question:

    1. Mahdokht writes about the importance of peace in the world. How do you feel about war and peace in the world?

C. Write about war and peace.

_____

_____

_____

_____

_____

_____

_____

D. Read your story to a partner. Ask your partner a question about her or his story.

State and Local Government

7. Take the Test

This section will give you practice for the Naturalization Test.

CD 2
Track 4

A. Listen to the questions. Circle the correct answers. Fill in the information about your city and state.

1. What is the chief executive of a state government called?

   a. mayor
   b. governor

   c. city manager
   d. president

2. What is one power of the states?

   a. to make laws about war
   b. to provide schooling and education

   c. to set up the postal system
   d. to set up the federal courts

3. What is the chief executive of a city called?

   a. mayor
   b. governor

   c. judge
   d. president

4. Who is the governor of our state?

   _____

5. Who is the chief executive of our local government?

   _____

6. What is the capital of our state?

   _____

7. What is one power of our local government?

   a. to provide health care services
   b. to print money

   c. to declare war
   d. to make treaties

8. What is the highest court in our state?

   _____

CD 2
Track 5

B. Now, listen again and check your answers.
Review the questions and answers with your partner. (Answers are at the back of the book on page 167.)

C. Listen to each sentence. Then, listen again and write what you hear. Fill in the information about your city and state.

1. _____

2. _____

3. _____

4. _____

5. _____

6. _____

Pairs: Check your partner's answers with the sentences on page 167.

D. N-400 Part 10D: Your Moral Character Interview a partner. (See pages 106–110 in Unit 10 for additional questions.)

1. Have you ever been placed in an alternative sentencing or a rehabilitative program?

2. Have you ever received a suspended sentence, been placed on probation, or been paroled?

3. Have you ever been in jail or prison?

4. Have you ever

   a. been a habitual drunkard?

   b. been a prostitute or procured anyone for prostitution?

   c. sold or smuggled controlled substances, illegal drugs, or narcotics?

   d. been married to more than one person at the same time?

   e. helped anyone enter or try to enter the United States illegally?

   f. gambled illegally or received income from illegal gambling?

   g. failed to support your dependents or to pay alimony?

5. Have you ever lied to or given false or misleading information to any U.S. government official while applying for any immigration benefit?

E. Clarification: If you don't understand something in the interview, you can say: *Excuse me. Did you say* where*? Or* When

8. Think About Your Learning

My favorite activity in this unit was _____ .

I want to study more about:

❏ State Government

❏ Local Government

❏ _____ (other)

9. Game

	What country do we live in? Spell it. →	What is the name of this city or town? Spell it.	Is there a city council in this area?	FINISH ★ ★ ★
↑	Who is the chief executive of our local government?	What is the highest court called in our state?	What is the legislature called in our state?	What is one power of the states? ← ↑
Which branch of state government makes the laws? ↑	What does the governor do? →		Who is the governor of our state?	How does our state raise money?
	Name the three branches of state government.	Does our state have its own government?	Does our state have its own constitution?	What is the abbreviation for our state? ← ↑
START ★ ★ ★ →	What is our state's name? Spell it.	What is our state's capital? Spell it.	What year was our state admitted to the Union?	

Unit 10
Becoming a Citizen

Naturalization Ceremony

Unit Focus

☆ Requirements to Become a Citizen

☆ Benefits and Rights of U.S. Citizens

☆ Responsibilities of U.S. Citizens

☆ The USCIS Interview

☆ Spotlight Reading: César Chávez

Key Vocabulary Preview

citizen	USCIS (U.S. Citizenship and Immigration Services)	community group	register
resident	Application for Naturalization (N-400 Form)	political issues	vote
nonresident	USCIS "A" Number	pay taxes	leave the U.S.
good moral character	Selective Service Registration	obey laws	re-enter the U.S.
loyalty	fingerprints	U.S. Passport	allegiance
	Lawful Permanent Resident	serve on a jury	Oath of Allegianc

1. **Before You Read**

A. Sit in a group of four. Look at the picture. Talk about the question below. Write your answers on the lines.

What are some things a citizen of the United States can do?

_____vote for president_____   _____   _____

_____   _____   _____

_____   _____   _____

B. Find out about your classmates. Fill in the chart.

Why do you think you will be a good citizen of the United States?

Name	Why?
Martha	She goes to community meetings and tries to make things better.

C. Read your ideas to the class.

EXAMPLE: Martha will be a good citizen because she goes to community meetings and tries to make things better.

2. Citizenship Reading

A. What do you know about these words? Write your ideas on the lines.

United States
Citizen

B. Read.

U.S. Citizenship: Requirements, Rights, and Responsibilities

	Requirements to Become a Citizen
Age	1. You must be 18 years old or older.
Residency	2. You must be a Lawful Permanent Resident for five years. **OR** 3. You must be a Lawful Permanent Resident for three years if your husband or wife has been a citizen for three years and you have been living with your spouse.
Literacy and Knowledge	4. You must understand, speak, read, and write simple English. (There are some exceptions.) 5. You will be asked questions about the information on your Application for Naturalization, the N-400 form. 6. You must pass an examination of U.S. government and history (civics) based on the U.S. Citizenship and Immigration Services (USCIS) 100 questions. 7. You will be asked to read and write sentences in English. You must pass a short dictation test.
Selective Service Registration	8. At the age of 18, all men must register for the Selective Service. All men between the ages of 18 and 26 are required to register for the Selective Service.
Loyalty	9. You must be willing to protect the United States.
Documents	10. You must file the N-400 form and other necessary documents, medical reports, fingerprints, and photographs with the USCIS.

Becoming a Citizen

Benefits and Rights of U.S. Citizens

- Register and vote in elections.
- Petition to bring family members permanently to the United States.
- Obtain citizenship for children born abroad.
- Travel with a U.S. passport.
- Work for federal government agencies and on jobs limited to citizens.
- Run for elected office.
- Leave and re-enter the United States without difficulty.
- Receive some financial aid and scholarships limited to U.S. Citizens.

Responsibilities of U.S. Citizens

- Swear allegiance to the United States. Give up allegiance to any other nation or government.
- Support and defend the Constitution and laws of the United States.
- Serve the country as required by law.
- Register and vote in elections.
- Serve on a jury.
- Respect the rights and opinions of others.
- Be an active community member. Give your opinions. (Join a civic or a community group.)
- Be of good moral character.
- Pay taxes. (April 15 is the last day to send in federal income tax forms.)
- Obey the laws.

C. Read the information again. Circle any new words. Add these words to your dictionary. Discuss the new words with your teacher and your classmates.

3. After You Read

A. Fill in the blanks with the words below. Read the story with a classmate.

history	~~18~~	write	questions	Lawful
vote	taxes	obey	moral	N-400
opinion	April 15	register		

You need to be (1) _____ 18 _____ years old to become a naturalized citizen of the United States. In general, you must be a (2) _____ Permanent Resident for five years before you can be a citizen. You need to understand, speak, read, and (3) _____ English. All men between the ages of 18 and 26 must (4) _____ for the Selective Service.

The examination you will take is about U.S. (5) _____ and government. There are 100 possible (6) _____ . You must fill out a USCIS Application for Naturalization called the (7) _____ form. You will be interviewed about the information on this form. A person applying for citizenship must be of good (8) _____ character.

A citizen is responsible for paying (9) _____ . The last day to send in federal income tax forms is (10) _____ . Also, a citizen must (11) _____ the law. A citizen learns about the issues at a local, state, and national level. After that, a citizen can (12) _____ responsibly in an election. Giving an elected official your (13) _____ on an issue is one way to participate in a democracy.

César Chávez
1927–1993

César Chávez was a Mexican American born during the Depression. When he was 10, his family lost their land in Arizona and became migrant workers (people who move to different places to find work).

The Chávez family worked in fields and vineyards in the Southwest picking fruits and vegetables. It was a difficult life. They had very little money. Their living and working conditions were dirty and dangerous. They lived in migrant camps and sometimes they slept in their car. César went to more than thirty elementary schools. While he was at school, he often experienced discrimination.

César became a union organizer in 1952. He traveled around California and urged Mexican Americans to register and vote. After that, he moved with his wife, Helen, and eight children to Delano, California. César Chávez and Dolores Huerta began to organize farm workers. They founded the National Farm Workers Association (NFWA). They demanded higher pay from the growers.

In 1965, the NFWA, joined a strike against Delano grape growers. They got people all over the United States to support the farm workers and to boycott (stop buying) grapes. Robert Kennedy supported Chávez. Students, church groups, minorities, and consumers supported the farm workers. Later, NFWA became the United Farm Workers (UFW).

In the 1970s and 1980s, the UFW organized strikes for higher pay for farm workers. César led boycotts to stop the use of toxic pesticides on grapes. As a result of the work of César Chávez, Dolores Huerta, and the UFW, many farm workers got contracts with living wages and better working conditions.

During his lifetime, César continued to work for the rights of farm workers. In 1994, after his death, his wife received the Presidential Medal of Freedom in his honor. The award was presented at the White House by President Bill Clinton. In 2002, the U.S. Postal Service issued a stamp commemorating the influence César Chávez had on American life.

5. Make It Real

A. In your USCIS interview, you'll be asked to raise your right hand and swear that you promise to tell the truth. You'll say, "I do." Practice this with your teacher and classmates.

B. Preparing for Your USCIS Interview: Practice answering these general questions with your teacher and classmates.

- ★ How are you today?
- ★ What colors are your clothes?
- ★ How did you get here today?
- ★ What are you wearing today?

- ★ Tell me about the weather today.
- ★ Where did you study English?
- ★ Who was your teacher in the citizenship program?

C. These are the additional N-400 questions. Practice them with your teacher and classmates. (See the N-400 Form at the back of the book.)

- ★ Walk around the classroom.
- ★ Ask each student one question.
- ★ Move to another student and ask a different question.

> **1. NAME, ADDRESS, AND ELIGIBILITY QUESTIONS**
>
> a. What's your current legal name?
> b. What's your home address?
> c. What's your birth date?
> d. What's your telephone number?
> e. What's your USCIS "A" number?

> **2. MORE ELIGIBILITY QUESTIONS**
>
> a. What is your Social Security Number?
> b. Are you a Lawful Permanent Resident?
> c. How long have you been a Lawful Permanent Resident?
> d. When and where did you enter the United States?
> e. Of what country are you a citizen?
> f. Have you used any other name since you became a Lawful Permanent Resident?
> g. Are you single, married, divorced, or widowed?
> h. Have you ever been absent from the United States since you became a Lawful Permanent Resident?
> i. How many times have you left the country?
> j. When and why were you absent?
> k. Were you absent for more than six months at any time?
> l. Are you asking for a waiver of the naturalization process because of a disability?

- ★ Sit in a group of three.
- ★ Student A asks the first four questions.
- ★ Student B asks the next four questions.
- ★ Student C asks the final four questions.

* ★ Sit with a partner.
* ★ Student A is the applicant.
* ★ Student B is the USCIS interviewer.
* ★ Interview your partner.
* ★ Then change roles.

3. PHYSICAL DESCRIPTION AND RESIDENCE QUESTIONS

a. How tall are you?
b. How much do you weigh?
c. What is your race?
d. What color is your hair?
e. What color are your eyes?
f. How long have you lived at your present address?
g. Where did you live before?

4. EMPLOYMENT AND EDUCATION QUESTIONS

a. How long have you worked at your present job?
b. What is your position?
c. What did you do on your last job?
d. How long did you work there?
e. Why did you leave your last job?
f. What school did you attend in the last five years?
g. What do you study in school?

* ★ Walk around the classroom.
* ★ Ask a student the questions.
* ★ Move to another student and ask the questions again.

* ★ Sit in a group of four.
* ★ Each student selects three questions.
* ★ Write each question on a separate piece of paper.
* ★ Put the pieces of paper in a bag.
* ★ Draw a question from the bag.
* ★ Answer the question.

5. MARITAL HISTORY QUESTIONS

a. Are you married now?
b. How many times have you been married?
c. What is the name of your husband or wife?
d. What is his or her date of birth?
e. Where was he or she born?
f. What is his or her citizenship?
g. What is his or her Social Security Number?
h. Is your wife or husband a naturalized citizen?
i. What was the name of your previous spouse?
j. How long were you married?

- ★ Sit in a group of four.
- ★ Study the questions.
- ★ Answer one question.
  Example: My son was born on May 15, 1986.
- ★ The other students look at the list and find the correct question.

6. QUESTIONS ABOUT CHILDREN

a. What is the name and age of your child (children)?
b. What is the birth date of your child?
c. Where was your child born?
d. What country is your child a citizen of?
e. What is your child's USCIS "A" number??
f. Where does your child live?
g. Who supports your child?

7. GENERAL QUESTIONS

a. Have you ever claimed to be a U.S. citizen in writing or any other way?
b. Have you ever registered to vote in any Federal, state, or local election in the United States?
c. Have you ever voted in any Federal, state, or local election in the United States?
d. Since becoming a Lawful Permanent Resident, have you ever failed to file a required Federal, state, or local tax return?
e. Do you owe any Federal, state, or local taxes that are overdue?
f. Have you ever been declared legally incompetent or been confined to a mental institution within the last five years?

- ★ Sit in a group of three.
- ★ In each question, circle key vocabulary words.
- ★ Make a list of the words and discuss them.

- ★ Sit in a group of three.
- ★ In each question, circle key vocabulary words.
- ★ Make a list of the words and discuss them.

8. QUESTIONS ABOUT AFFILIATIONS

a. Have you ever been a member of or associated with any organization, fund, foundation, club, or similar group in the United States or in any other place?
b. Have you ever been a member of or in any way associated with the Communist Party? A totalitarian party? A terrorist organization?
c. Have you ever advocated the overthrow of any government by force or violence?
d. Have you ever persecuted any person because of race, religion, national origin, or membership in a particular social group or political opinion?
e. Between March 23, 1933, and May 8, 1945, did you work for or associate in any way with the Nazi government of Germany or any of its affiliates?

Becoming a Citizen

9. QUESTIONS ABOUT RESIDENCY AND MORAL CHARACTER

★ Talk to your teacher and classmates about how you would answer these questions and why.

a. Since becoming a Lawful Permanent Resident of the United States, have you ever called yourself a "nonresident" on a Federal, state, or local tax return?

b. Have you ever failed to file a Federal, state, or local tax return because you considered yourself to be a "nonresident"?

c. Have you ever committed a crime or offense for which you were not arrested?

d. Have you ever been arrested, cited, or detained by any law enforcement officer (including USCIS or military officers) for any reason?

e. Have you ever been charged with committing any crime or offense?

f. Have you ever been convicted of a crime or offense?

10. MORE QUESTIONS ABOUT MORAL CHARACTER

a. Have you ever been placed in an alternative sentencing or a rehabilitative program?

b. Have you ever received a suspended sentence, been placed on probation, or been paroled?

c. Have you ever been in jail or prison?

d. Have you ever been a habitual drunkard?

e. Have you ever been a prostitute or procured anyone for prostitution?

f. Have you ever sold or smuggled controlled substances, illegal drugs, or narcotics?

g. Have you ever been married to more than one person at the same time?

h. Have you ever helped anyone enter or try to enter the United States illegally?

i. Have you ever gambled illegally or received income from illegal gambling?

j. Have you ever failed to support your dependents or to pay alimony?

k. Have you ever lied to or given false or misleading information to any U.S. government official while applying for any immigration benefit?

★ Talk to your teacher and classmates about how you would answer these questions and why.

11. MILITARY SERVICE QUESTIONS

★ Talk to your teacher and classmates about how you would answer these questions and why.

a. Have you ever been removed or deported from the United States?

b. Have you ever served in the U.S. Armed Forces?

c. Have you ever deserted the U.S. Armed Forces?

d. What is your Selective Service Number?

e. When did you register with the Selective Service?

12. ALLEGIANCE TO THE UNITED STATES QUESTIONS

a. Do you support the Constitution and the form of government of the United States?

b. Are you willing to take the full Oath of Allegiance to the United States?

c. Are you willing to bear arms on behalf of the United States?

d. Are you willing to perform noncombatant services in the Armed Forces?

e. Are you willing to perform work of national importance under civilian direction?

★ Discuss the questions with your classmates and teacher.

★ Find a partner.

★ Practice the questions.

6. Real Stories

A. Read a student's story.

My Citizenship Interview

This week, I had my citizenship interview. I felt very nervous. The interviewer was very friendly. He told me not to worry. I asked him if he could ask the U.S. history and government questions first, so I wouldn't forget the answers. He agreed. He asked, "What was the first holiday the Pilgrims celebrated?" He asked about the color of the stars in the flag. I got those answers right! After that, he asked questions about my N-400 application form. He asked, "Where do you live? How long have you lived there? Where do you work? What's your job?" Later, he asked me to read a sentence and then he dictated a sentence for me to write.

When he told me I passed the test, I felt proud. He gave me a congratulatory letter. Tonight I came to talk to my citizenship class. The study and practice we do every week in our citizenship class is very helpful. I told the students, "I had a good experience. If you practice, you can pass the citizenship interview, too."

Jania Sanchez

B. Talk to a classmate about these questions:
1. How did Jania feel on the day of the test?
2. How do you think you will feel on the day of your test?
3. What does it mean to you to be a citizen?

C. Write a story about becoming a citizen.

_____

_____

_____

_____

D. Read your story to a partner. Ask your partner a question about his or her story.

7. Take the Test

This section will give you practice for the Naturalization Test.

CD 2
Track 7

A. Listen to the questions and possible answers. Circle the correct answers.

1. What Immigration and Naturalization form is used to apply to become a naturalized citizen?

   a. N-200   **c.** N-400
   b. I-158   **d.** USCIS 505

2. What is one responsibility that is only for U.S. citizens?

   a. serve on a jury   **c.** study English
   b. work at a hospital   **d.** read a book at the library

3. What are two rights only for U.S. citizens?

   a. pay taxes and go to the library   **c.** work hard and give an opinion
   b. vote in a federal election   **d.** work hard and study English
      and apply for a federal job

4. What are two ways that Americans can participate in their democracy? (Circle two answers.)

   a. Join a community group.   **c.** Go shopping and spend money.
   b. Vote.   **d.** Read a book at the library.

5. When is the last day you can send in federal income tax forms?

   a. January 1   **c.** July 4
   b. April 15   **d.** May 31

6. When must all men register for the Selective Service?

   a. at the age of 16   **c.** at the age of 18
   b. at the age of 21   **d.** at the age of 25

7. You must be _____ years old or older to become a naturalized citizen.

   a. 21   **c.** 16
   b. 18   **d.** 14

8. What is the literacy requirement?

   You must understand, _____ , read, and write simple English.

CD 2
Track 8

B. Now, listen again and check your answers.
Review the questions and answers with your partner. (Answers are at the back of the book on page 168.)

112 ★ Unit Ten

Becoming a Citizen

C. Listen to each sentence. Then, listen again and write what you hear.

1. _____

2. _____

3. _____

4. _____

5. _____

Pairs: Check your partner's answers with the sentences on page 168.

D. Clarification: When someone asks you to sign the form, if you don't know where to sign, you can ask: *Where do I sign my name?*

8. **Think About Your Learning**

My favorite activity in this unit was _____ .

I want to study more about:

❏ Becoming a Citizen

❏ Benefits, Rights, and Responsibilities of U.S. Citizens

❏ The USCIS Interview

❏ _____ (other)

Appendix A

Introduction to the Beginning Level Pages

The following pages are designed to familiarize the beginning level student with citizenship material.

Suggested Teaching Procedures

1. The teacher sets the context of the lesson by using pictures and words.

   EXAMPLE: "Today we're going to talk about Thanksgiving. Do you know when Thanksgiving is?"

   The teacher holds up a picture of a turkey and a calendar with Thanksgiving Day circled on the calendar.

2. The teacher has students focus on the images on the page. The teacher asks, "What do you see in Picture 2?" Students respond with words: "water, a ship." The teacher rephrases and says, "That's right. The Pilgrims sailed across the water on a ship called the Mayflower."

3. The teacher and students look at the other pictures on the page. The teacher asks, "What do you see in Picture 3? In Picture 4?" After each question, the teacher rephrases student responses into keywords and sentences.

4. The teacher reads the key words and sentences slowly to the class. The students look at the pictures. Before reading each sentence, the teacher says the picture number.

   EXAMPLE: Picture 1: The Pilgrims leave England for religious freedom.
   Picture 2: They sail on the *Mayflower*.

   (This process may be repeated several times.)

5. The teacher reads the sentences again. Students point to the pictures.

6. To focus on vocabulary, the teacher says, "Point to the Pilgrims in Picture 1. Point to the *Mayflower* in Picture 2."

7. The teacher reads the sentences with the students. (The teacher may repeat this step.)

8. Student pairs practice pointing to the pictures. They practice reading the words and sentences together.

To Focus on Listening

★ The teacher pronounces key words. Students point to the corresponding pictures.

★ The teacher pronounces key words in random order. Students circle the words under the pictures.

To Focus on Reading and Speaking

★ Students practice reading the sentences with a classmate.

★ One student points to a picture. Another student reads the corresponding sentence.

To Focus on Writing

★ Students copy the key words and sentences.

★ Students practice spelling the words with a classmate.

★ The teacher dictates the key words or sentences.

★ Partners dictate the key words or sentences to each other.

★ Students compare their writing to the sentences in Section B in each of the Beginning Level units.

Beginning Level Pages

Unit 1

A. Look at the pictures. Look at the words under the pictures.

1
- Pilgrims
- England
- religious freedom

2
- sail
- *Mayflower*

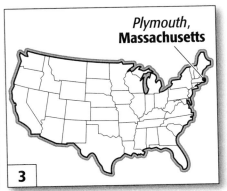

3
- arrive
- Plymouth, Massachusetts
- 1620

4
- American Indians (Native Americans)
- teach
- plant, hunt, fish

5
- celebrate
- first Thanksgiving

6
- fourth Thursday
- November

B. Look at the pictures again. Listen to your teacher read the sentences. Read with your class. Copy the sentences.

1. The Pilgrims leave England for religious freedom.
2. They sail on the *Mayflower.*
3. They arrive at Plymouth, Massachusetts, in 1620.
4. American Indians (Native Americans) teach Pilgrims to plant, hunt, and fish.
5. The Pilgrims and the American Indians (Native Americans) celebrate the first Thanksgiving.
6. Thanksgiving is the fourth Thursday in November.

Unit 2

A. Look at the pictures. Look at the words under the pictures.

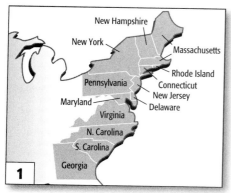

- 13 colonies

- English
- tax
- tea, stamps, sugar

- colonists
- Declaration of Independence
- 1776

- American Revolution
- 1783

- George Washington
- President

- July 4
- Independence Day

B. Look at the pictures again. Listen to your teacher read the sentences. Read with your class. Copy the sentences.

1. There are 13 colonies.
2. The English tax tea, stamps, and sugar.
3. Colonists sign the Declaration of Independence in 1776.
4. The colonists win the American Revolution in 1783.
5. George Washington is the first President of the United States.
6. July 4 is Independence Day.

Unit 3

A. Look at the pictures. Look at the words under the pictures.

- Constitution
- supreme law

- Bill of Rights
- amendments

- freedom of speech
- say
- think

- freedom of assembly
- meet
- group

- freedom of religion
- practice
- religion

- freedom of press
- publish
- ideas

B. Look at the pictures again. Listen to your teacher read the sentences. Read with your class. Copy the sentences.

1. The Constitution is the supreme law of the land.
2. The Bill of Rights is the first ten amendments to the Constitution.
3. Freedom of speech is the right to say what you think.
4. Freedom of assembly is the right to meet in a group.
5. Freedom of religion is the right to practice religion.
6. Freedom of press is the right to publish your ideas.

Unit 4

A. Look at the pictures. Look at the words under the pictures.

- African slaves
- America
- chains

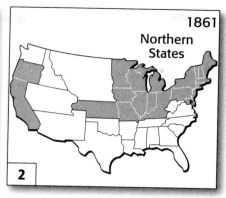

- Northern states
- workers
- free

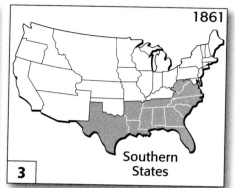

- Southern states
- slaves

- Abraham Lincoln
- President
- 1861–1865

- soldiers
- Civil War

- Emancipation Proclamation
- frees the slaves

B. Look at the pictures again. Listen to your teacher read the sentences. Read with your class. Copy the sentences.

1. African slaves come to America in chains.
2. Northern states want workers to be free.
3. Southern states want slaves.
4. Abraham Lincoln is President from 1861 to 1865.
5. Northern soldiers win the Civil War.
6. The Emancipation Proclamation frees the slaves.

Unit 5

A. Look at the pictures. Look at the words under the pictures.

- workers
- better conditions
- 1900

- World War I
- 1914–1918

- women
- vote
- 1920

- Depression
- no money

- World War II
- 1939–1945

- Dr. Martin Luther King, Jr.
- equality
- 1929–1968

B. Look at the pictures again. Listen to your teacher read the sentences. Read with your class. Copy the sentences.

1. Workers want better working conditions in 1900.
2. World War I is from 1914 to 1918.
3. Women vote in 1920.
4. In the Depression, people have no money.
5. World War II is from 1939 to 1945.
6. Dr. Martin Luther King, Jr. wants equality for all people. He lives from 1929 to 1968.

Unit 6

A. Look at the pictures. Look at the words under the pictures.

1
- flag
- United States

2
- Statue of Liberty
- New York Harbor

3
- July 4
- Independence Day

4
- right hand
- heart

5
- pledge allegiance
- flag

6
- "The Star-Spangled Banner"
- national song

B. Look at the pictures again. Listen to your teacher read the sentences. Read with your class. Copy the sentences.

1. The United States flag has 50 stars and 13 stripes.
2. The Statue of Liberty is in New York Harbor.
3. July 4 is Independence Day.
4. Put your right hand over your heart.
5. Say, "I pledge allegiance to the flag...."
6. "The Star-Spangled Banner" is the national song.

Unit 7

A. Look at the pictures. Look at the words under the pictures.

- legislative branch
- makes laws

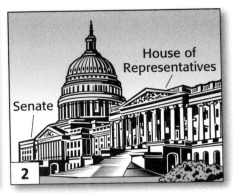

- Senate
- House of Representatives

- Capitol Building
- Washington, D.C.

- 100
- senators

- 435
- representatives

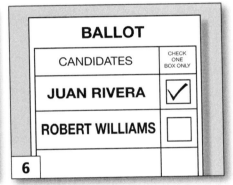

- vote for
- senators and representatives

B. Look at the pictures again. Listen to your teacher read the sentences. Read with your class. Copy the sentences.

1. The legislative branch makes the laws.
2. The Senate and the House of Representatives are two parts of the legislative branch.
3. Members of the Senate and the House meet in the Capitol Building in Washington, D.C.
4. There are 100 senators.
5. There are 435 representatives.
6. We vote for senators and representatives.

Unit 8

A. Look at the pictures. Look at the words under the pictures.

- Election Day
- November

- White House

- President
- can sign and veto laws

- leader
- country

- nine justices
- Supreme Court

- justices
- listen to
- decide court cases

B. Look at the pictures again. Listen to your teacher read the sentences. Read with your class. Copy the sentences.

1. Election Day is in November.
2. The White House is where the president lives and works.
3. The president can sign and veto laws.
4. The president is the leader of the country.
5. There are nine justices on the Supreme Court.
6. The justices listen to and decide court cases.

Unit 9

A. Look at the picture. Look at the words under the picture.

Congresswoman Maxine Waters

1. _____ is the name of this state.	**2.** _____ is the capital of this state.	**3.** _____ is the governor of this state.
4. She/He is a _____. (political party)	**5.** My state senator is _____.	**6.** He/She is a _____. (political party)
7. My state representative is _____.	**8.** She/He is a _____. (political party)	**9.** _____ is the name of this city.
10. _____ is the mayor/manager of this city.	**11.** He/She is a _____. (political party)	

B. Read the sentences with your classmates. Practice spelling your answers.

Unit 10

A. Look at the pictures. Listen to your teacher read. Point to the pictures.

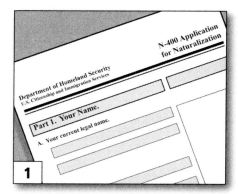

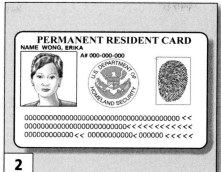

B. Look at the words. Listen to the teacher read the words. Match the words with the correct picture. Read the words with a classmate.

_____ Permanent Resident card

_____ marriage certificate

_____ Social Security card

_____ fingerprints

_____ driver's license

_____ Selective Service papers

_____ personal photos

_____ N-400 Form

Appendix B

Community and Civics Participation Projects

Unit 1   Building Your School Community

Objective

You want to find out about the people who work at your school.

Class Activity

Make a team of four or five students. With your team, decide who you want to interview: the school principal (director), the assistant principal, the school counselor, the school receptionist, the school secretary, the bookstore director, the computer teacher, or the school custodian. Make a list of questions to ask that person.

★ Name?

★ Hours of work?

★ Job Duties?

★ Why is the job important?

Ask your teacher to review the questions.

Interview the person. Ask questions. Take notes.

Group Sharing

Meet with your group. Talk about what you learned from the person about her or his job and why it is important. Select a reporter. The reporter reports the information to the class.

Class Presentation

Reporters: Use your notes. Tell the class the name of the person you talked to and what his or her job is at your school. Tell your class why that person's work is important to your school.

Unit 2   Doing a Community Walk, Mapping Your Community

Objective

You want to find out about the neighborhood around your school.

Class Activity

Take a walking field trip with your teacher and classmates in the neighborhood around your school. Create a map. Draw your school and write the name of your school. Show any nearby houses and apartment buildings and their addresses. Show the library. List the names of businesses and their addresses on the map. Show the main streets. Put in the stoplights, stop signs, bus stops, and railroad crossings. Show the parks and community centers.

Group Sharing

Make a group of four. Come back to your classroom and share your community map with your group. Compare your map with other student's maps. Fill in any missing information. Talk with the other students in your group about how you come to school.

★ How far is the school from your home?
★ Do you walk to school, drive, or take the bus?
★ Do you come to school alone or with a family member or friend?
★ How long does it take you to come to school?
★ What streets do you take to come to school?

Class Presentation

Use your Community Map. Explain to your class how you come to school.

Extension

How can you get from your house to the community health clinic?

★ To the library?
★ To the community center?
★ To the senior center?

Unit 3   Using the Public Library

Objective

You want to find out about your public library and the services it offers. You want to get a library card and check out books. You want to bring children to the library.

Class Activity: Library Card

First, go to the library and get an application for a library card. Fill in your name, address, city, zip code, and other information. (Bring some other identification with you to confirm where you live.) Turn in your library card application form. Get a library card.

Class Activity: At the Library

Walk around and look at the books. Find the English as a Second Language section. Find the Children's section. Find the encyclopedias. Find the magazines and newspapers. Find a book and check it out. Find out what the fees are if you return the book late.

Get a copy of the library schedule. When do they have children's story time? When do they have Internet classes? When do they have adult Literacy classes?

Find out how to sign in on the library computers. Get an e-mail address. Or, log in on the computer and see if you have any e-mail messages.

Class Sharing

Discuss your experience at the library and how it can help you learn more about the United States and the world. Talk about when you will bring your children or other members of your family to the library.

Unit 4   Finding Out About Community Protection Agencies, Reporting Emergencies

Objective

You want to find out the addresses and telephone numbers of the police department and fire department in your neighborhood. You want to know how to report an emergency.

Class Activity

Take a field trip to the fire department and talk with the firefighters. Or, take a field trip to the police department and talk with the police. Ask questions about their training and their jobs. Find out how firefighters help people who are victims of fires. Find out how to report an emergency. What opportunities are there to volunteer and work with firefighters? Find out how the police help people in your community to be safe. What opportunities are there to volunteer and work with the police?

Class Sharing

Talk about what you learned from the firefighters and the police. Talk about how to report an emergency. Would you like to do volunteer work with them? Why or why not? What can you do to make your community a safer place?

Unit 5   Finding Out About Community Resources

Objective

You want to find out about the community resource agencies in your area.

Class Activity

First, talk with your teacher and classmates about where the elementary schools, middle schools, high schools, adult education programs, health care centers, senior centers, and community service agencies are in your community. Find out what services or classes each offers.

To help in your search:

> ★ Read the government pages and the business pages of the telephone book.
> ★ Look up each agency's name on the Internet. Read about the agency.
> ★ Call the agency and ask questions about what they do and if they offer free services. If the services are not free, ask how much their services cost.

Class Project

Make a list of community resource agencies and the services each agency provides. Make copies for everyone in your class.

At Home

Keep the list of community resource agencies and the services they provide next to your telephone.

Community and Civics Participation Projects

Unit 6   Using the Banking System

Objective

You want to set up a bank account at a bank in your community. You want to find out what banking services are available.

Class Activity

Find a bank near your school. Invite one of the bank officers to your class to talk about banking services.

With your teacher and classmates, make a list of questions you want to ask.
- ★ Find out about the kinds of accounts the bank offers: savings, checking, ATM card, debit card, or credit card.
- ★ Find out about the interest paid by the bank.
- ★ Ask about how to use an ATM (Automatic Teller Machine).
- ★ Ask about how you can maintain credit card safety.
- ★ Ask about the minimum deposit required in a checking account.
- ★ Ask about the minimum deposit required in a savings account.
- ★ Find out what "good credit" means. Find out why it is important to have "good credit."
- ★ Find out how to read a bank statement.

Listen to the bank officer give the presentation. Ask your questions. Take some notes. Be prepared to talk about the information.

Group and Class Sharing

Talk about what you learned about the services offered at the bank. Would you like to open a bank account? Why or why not?

Unit 7   Civic Participation: Participating in Community Events

Objective

You want to attend and participate in a community meeting. You want to learn about your rights to freedom of assembly and freedom of speech.

Class Activity

Read the local newspaper to find out about community meetings and events. Look for community meetings on the Internet. City council meetings, PTA (Parent Teacher Association) meetings, neighborhood meetings, town hall meetings, library association and political organization meetings are all listed in the newspaper.

Decide which meeting you want to attend. Look for the date, time, and location of the meeting. What is the meeting about?

Go to the meeting with some of your classmates. Listen to the discussion. Give your ideas or opinions about the issues. When you attend a meeting, listen to the issues, and voice your opinion, you are participating in your community!

Group and Class Sharing

Talk about these questions with your group, your teacher, and your classmates.

★ What was discussed at the meeting?

★ Who was talking?

★ What did the person say?

★ What is your opinion?

Unit 8   Civic Participation: Participating in an Election for Class Representative

Objective

You want to learn about voting in the United States. You want to participate in the voting process.

Class Activity

First, find out the issues that are important to students in your class (the class schedule, the cleanliness of the school, student recognition and student awards, child care, counseling services, etc.). Have students who want to be elected as class representatives give speeches about how they will represent their classmates' ideas on the issues.

After all the candidates have spoken, your class will discuss the ideas of each candidate. Then, the class will hold an election for class representative or student council representative. Each student in the class votes for the person they want to be their elected representative.

Class Sharing

Following this lesson, talk about who you will vote for in the next national or state election and why.

Unit 9   Civic Participation: Visiting a Local or State Representative

Objective

You want to meet your local or state representative and find out their ideas.

Class Activity

First, find out the name, local address, telephone number, and e-mail address of your representative. Call and make an appointment to meet with the representative (or have them visit your class.)

With your teacher and classmates, talk about any problems in your community (broken stop lights, dirty streets, lack of personal safety, noise, bad schools, etc.). Make a list of questions you want to ask about community problems.

Listen to the representative give his or her presentation. Ask your questions. While the representative is talking, take some notes on the chart. Be prepared to talk about the information you hear.

Name of Representative _____	**Today's Date** _____	
Office Address _____	**Office Phone Number** _____	
Notes: _____		
_____		

Class Sharing

Talk about what you learned from your representative about your community. With your teacher and classmates, make a plan about what you can do to help solve community problems. Talk about how your representative's office can help you with your plan.

Unit 10   Goal Setting: Setting Educational and Career Goals

Objective

You want to make plans for your future job.

Individual/Group Research

Decide what job you would like to have in the future. Form a group with other students in your class who are interested in the same kind of job. Search for information about the job in the U.S. Department of Labor's *Occupational Outlook Handbook* and online at: http://www.bls.gov/oco/ocos069.htm
Find out about:

- ★ the job duties and responsibilities
- ★ how much education and training is required
- ★ how much money you will make
- ★ what schedule you will work
- ★ if the job will be full-time or part-time

Take notes on the information.

Individual Planning

Make an individual plan for your necessary education and training. Make a plan for getting the job. Determine:

- ★ how many years you will need to be in school
- ★ the reading level you will need
- ★ if you will need to have a GED or high school diploma

★ if you will need to go to college

★ if you will need to have training after college

★ who you can talk to for more information about the job

Group Sharing

Form a group of four. Share the information you find out with your group. Discuss the reasons why you want the job. Discuss some possible problems you might have with the job.

Class Sharing

Make a report to your class about the job, the salary, and the education and training required. Make a poster or write the information on the board. Tell the class why you want to have this job.

Bonus Activity: Using Timelines to Review U.S. History

Objective

You want to review important events in U.S. history.

Group Activity

Make a team of five to eight students. Decide if you want to review the events of the 1700s, the 1800s, or the 1900s in United States history. Select the appropriate timeline(s) from Units 1–5 of *U.S. Citizen, Yes*.

Take out some blank pieces of paper. On each piece of paper, write one important event and the date it happened.

EXAMPLE: World War II
             1939–1945

Put all the pieces of paper in one pile. Select one piece of paper and study that information. Review the reading section in the text and become an expert on your event.

Group Sharing

Group members: talk together about your event and the date(s) of the event. Ask each other questions.

Class Presentation

Make a line in front of the class with your teammates. Line up in chronological order (what happened first to what happened last). Explain your event and the date(s) of the event to the class.

EXAMPLE: World War II was from 1939 to 1945. The United States was allies with
             England, France, and Russia in World War II.

Class members take notes and ask questions.

100 Civics (History and Government) Questions for the Redesigned Naturalization Test

The 100 civics (history and government) questions and answers for the redesigned naturalization test are listed below.

Test yourself. Cover the answers with a sheet of paper, and try to answer the questions. Then practice asking and answering these questions with other students.

*If you are 65 years old or older and have been a legal permanent resident of the United States for 20 or more years, you may study just the questions that have been marked with an asterisk.

AMERICAN GOVERNMENT

A: Principles of American Democracy

CD 2
Track 10

1. **What is the supreme law of the land?**
   - *the Constitution*

2. **What does the Constitution do?**
   - *sets up the government*
   - *defines the government*
   - *protects the basic rights of Americans*

3. **The idea of self-government is in the first three words of the Constitution. What are these words?**
   - *We the People*

4. **What is an amendment?**
   - *a change (to the Constitution)*
   - *an addition (to the Constitution)*

5. **What do we call the first ten amendments to the Constitution?**
   - *the Bill of Rights*

6. **What is <u>one</u> right or freedom from the First Amendment?**
   - *speech*
   - *religion*
   - *assembly*
   - *press*
   - *petition the government*

7. **How many amendments does the Constitution have?**
   - *twenty-seven (27)*

8. **What did the Declaration of Independence do?**
   - *announced our independence (from Great Britain)*
   - *declared our independence (from Great Britain)*
   - *said that the United States is free (from Great Britain)*

9. **What are <u>two</u> rights in the Declaration of Independence?**
   - *life*
   - *liberty*
   - *pursuit of happiness*

10. **What is freedom of religion?**
   - *You can practice any religion, or not practice a religion.*

11. **What is the economic system in the United States?***
   - *capitalist economy*
   - *market economy*

12. **What is the "rule of law"?**
   - *Everyone must follow the law.*
   - *Leaders must obey the law.*
   - *Government must obey the law.*
   - *No one is above the law.*

B: System of Government

CD 2
Track 11

13. **Name <u>one</u> branch or part of the government.***
   - *Congress*
   - *legislative*
   - *President*
   - *executive*
   - *the courts*
   - *judicial*

14. **What stops <u>one</u> branch of government from becoming too powerful?**
   - *checks and balances*
   - *separation of powers*

15. **Who is in charge of the executive branch?**
   - *the President*

16. **Who makes federal laws?**
   - *Congress*
   - *Senate and House (of Representatives)*
   - *(U.S. or national) legislature*

17. **What are <u>two</u> parts of the U.S. Congress?***
   - *the Senate and House (of Representatives)*

18. **How many U.S. Senators are there?**
   - *one hundred (100)*

19. **We elect a U.S. Senator for how many years?**
   - *six (6)*

20. **Who is <u>one</u> of your state's U.S. Senators now?***
   - *Answers will vary. [District of Columbia residents and residents of U.S. territories should answer that D.C. (or the territory where the applicant lives) has no U.S. Senators.]*

21. **The House of Representatives has how many voting members?**
   - *four hundred thirty-five (435)*

22. **We elect a U.S. Representative for how many years?**
   - *two (2)*

23. **Name your U.S. Representative.**
   - *Answers will vary. [Residents of territories with nonvoting Delegates or Resident Commissioners may provide the name of that Delegate or Commissioner. Also acceptable is any statement that the territory has no (voting) Representatives in Congress.]*

24. **Who does a U.S. Senator represent?**
    - *all the people of the state*

25. **Why do some states have more Representatives than other states?**
    - *(because) of the state's population*
    - *(because) they have more people*
    - *(because) some states have more people*

26. **We elect a President for how many years?**
    - *four (4)*

27. **In what month do we vote for President?***
    - *November*

28. **What is the name of the President of the United States now?***
    - *Barack Obama*

29. **What is the name of the Vice President of the United States now?**
    - *Joe Biden*

30. **If the President can no longer serve, who becomes President?**
    - *the Vice President*

31. **If both the President and the Vice President can no longer serve, who becomes President?**
    - *the Speaker of the House*

32. **Who is the Commander in Chief of the military?**
    - *the President*

33. **Who signs bills to become laws?**
    - *the President*

34. **Who vetoes bills?**
    - *the President*

35. **What does the President's Cabinet do?**
    - *advises the President*

36. **What are two Cabinet-level positions?**
    - *Secretary of Agriculture*
    - *Secretary of Commerce*
    - *Secretary of Defense*
    - *Secretary of Education*
    - *Secretary of Energy*
    - *Secretary of Health and Human Services*
    - *Secretary of Homeland Security*
    - *Secretary of Housing and Urban Development*
    - *Secretary of Interior*
    - *Secretary of Labor*
    - *Secretary of State*
    - *Secretary of Transportation*
    - *Secretary of Treasury*
    - *Secretary of Veterans' Affairs*
    - *Attorney General*
    - *Vice President*

37. **What does the judicial branch do?**
    - *reviews the laws*
    - *explains the laws*

- *resolves disputes (disagreements)*
- *decides if a law goes against the Constitution*

38. **What is the highest court in the United States?**
    - *the Supreme Court*

39. **How many justices are on the Supreme Court?**
    - *nine (9)*

40. **Who is the Chief Justice of the United States?**
    - *John Roberts (John G. Roberts, Jr.)*

41. **Under our Constitution, some powers belong to the federal government. What is <u>one</u> power of the federal government?**
    - *to print money*
    - *to declare war*
    - *to create an army*
    - *to make treaties*

42. **Under our Constitution, some powers belong to the states. What is <u>one</u> power of the states?**
    - *provide schooling and education*
    - *provide protection (police)*
    - *provide safety (fire departments)*
    - *give a driver's license*
    - *approve zoning and land use*

43. **Who is the Governor of your state now?**
    - *Answers will vary. [District of Columbia residents should answer that D.C. does not have a Governor.]*

44. **What is the capital of your state?***
    - *Answers will vary. [District of Columbia residents should answer that D.C. is not a state and does not have a capital. Residents of U.S. territories should name the capital of the territory.]*

45. **What are the <u>two</u> major political parties in the United States?***
    - *Democratic and Republican*

46. **What is the political party of the President now?**
    - *Democratic*

47. **What is the name of the Speaker of the House of Representatives now?**
    - *Nancy Pelosi*

C: Rights and Responsibilities

CD 2
Track 12

48. **There are four amendments to the Constitution about who can vote. Describe <u>one</u> of them.**
    - *Citizens eighteen (18) and older (can vote).*
    - *You don't have to pay (a poll tax) to vote.*
    - *Any citizen can vote. (Women and men can vote.)*
    - *A male citizen of any race (can vote).*

49. **What is <u>one</u> responsibility that is only for United States citizens?***
    - *serve on a jury*
    - *vote in a federal election*

50. **Name <u>one</u> right only for United States citizens.**
    - *vote in a federal election*
    - *run for federal office*

51. **What are <u>two</u> rights of everyone living in the United States?**
- *freedom of expression*
- *freedom of speech*
- *freedom of assembly*
- *freedom to petition the government*
- *freedom of worship*
- *the right to bear arms*

52. **What do we show loyalty to when we say the Pledge of Allegiance?**
- *the United States*
- *the flag*

53. **What is <u>one</u> promise you make when you become a United States citizen?**
- *give up loyalty to other countries*
- *defend the Constitution and laws of the United States*
- *obey the laws of the United States*
- *serve in the U.S. military (if needed)*
- *serve (do important work for) the nation (if needed)*
- *be loyal to the United States*

54. **How old do citizens have to be to vote for President?***
- *eighteen (18) and older*

55. **What are <u>two</u> ways that Americans can participate in their democracy?**
- *vote*
- *join a political party*
- *help with a campaign*
- *join a civic group*
- *join a community group*
- *give an elected official your opinion on an issue*
- *call Senators and Representatives*
- *publicly support or oppose an issue or policy*
- *run for office*
- *write to a newspaper*

56. **When is the last day you can send in federal income tax forms?***
- *April 15*

57. **When must all men register for the Selective Service?**
- *at age eighteen (18)*
- *between eighteen (18) and twenty-six (26)*

AMERICAN HISTORY

A: Colonial Period and Independence

CD 2
Track 13

58. **What is <u>one</u> reason colonists came to America?**
- *freedom*
- *political liberty*
- *religious freedom*
- *economic opportunity*
- *practice their religion*
- *escape persecution*

59. **Who lived in America before the Europeans arrived?**
   - *Native Americans*
   - *American Indians*

60. **What group of people was taken to America and sold as slaves?**
   - *Africans*
   - *people from Africa*

61. **Why did colonists fight the British?**
   - *because of high taxes (taxation without representation)*
   - *because the British army stayed in their houses (boarding, quartering)*
   - *because they didn't have self-government*

62. **Who wrote the Declaration of Independence?**
   - *(Thomas) Jefferson*

63. **When was the Declaration of Independence adopted?**
   - *July 4, 1776*

64. **There were 13 original states. Name <u>three</u>.**
   - *New Hampshire*
   - *Massachusetts*
   - *Rhode Island*
   - *Connecticut*
   - *New York*
   - *New Jersey*
   - *Pennsylvania*
   - *Delaware*
   - *Maryland*
   - *Virginia*
   - *North Carolina*
   - *South Carolina*
   - *Georgia*

65. **What happened at the Constitutional Convention?**
   - *The Constitution was written.*
   - *The Founding Fathers wrote the Constitution.*

66. **When was the Constitution written?**
   - *1787*

67. **The Federalist Papers supported the passage of the U.S. Constitution. Name <u>one</u> of the writers.**
   - *(James) Madison*
   - *(Alexander) Hamilton*
   - *(John) Jay*
   - *Publius*

68. **What is <u>one</u> thing Benjamin Franklin is famous for?**
   - *U.S. diplomat*
   - *oldest member of the Constitutional Convention*
   - *first Postmaster General of the United States*
   - *writer of "Poor Richard's Almanac"*
   - *started the first free libraries*

69. **Who is the "Father of Our Country"?**
   - *(George) Washington*

70. **Who was the first President?***
   - *(George) Washington*

B: 1800s

71. **What territory did the United States buy from France in 1803?**
   - *the Louisiana Territory*
   - *Louisiana*

CD 2
Track 14

72. **Name <u>one</u> war fought by the United States in the 1800s.**
   - *War of 1812*
   - *Mexican-American War*
   - *Civil War*
   - *Spanish-American War*

73. **Name the U.S. war between the North and the South.**
   - *the Civil War*
   - *the War between the States*

74. **Name <u>one</u> problem that led to the Civil War.**
   - *slavery*
   - *economic reasons*
   - *states' rights*

75. **What was <u>one</u> important thing that Abraham Lincoln did?***
   - *freed the slaves (Emancipation Proclamation)*
   - *saved (or preserved) the Union*
   - *led the United States during the Civil War*

76. **What did the Emancipation Proclamation do?**
   - *freed the slaves*
   - *freed slaves in the Confederacy*
   - *freed slaves in the Confederate states*
   - *freed slaves in most Southern states*

77. **What did Susan B. Anthony do?**
   - *fought for women's rights*
   - *fought for civil rights*

C: Recent American History and Other Important Historical Information

78. **Name <u>one</u> war fought by the United States in the 1900s.***
   - *World War I*
   - *World War II*
   - *Korean War*
   - *Vietnam War*
   - *(Persian) Gulf War*

CD 2
Track 15

79. **Who was President during World War I?**
   - *(Woodrow) Wilson*

80. **Who was President during the Great Depression and World War II?**
   - *(Franklin) Roosevelt*

81. **Who did the United States fight in World War II?**
   - *Japan, Germany, and Italy*

82. **Before he was President, Eisenhower was a general. What war was he in?**
   - *World War II*

83. **During the Cold War, what was the main concern of the United States?**
   - *Communism*

84. **What movement tried to end racial discrimination?**
   - *civil rights (movement)*

85. **What did Martin Luther King, Jr. do?***
   - *fought for civil rights*
   - *worked for equality of all Americans*

86. **What major event happened on September 11, 2001, in the United States?**
   - *Terrorists attacked the United States.*

87. **Name <u>one</u> American Indian tribe in the United States.**
   - *Cherokee*
   - *Navajo*
   - *Sioux*
   - *Chippewa*
   - *Choctaw*
   - *Pueblo*
   - *Apache*
   - *Iroquois*
   - *Creek*
   - *Blackfeet*
   - *Seminole*
   - *Cheyenne*
   - *Arawak*
   - *Shawnee*
   - *Mohegan*
   - *Huron*
   - *Oneida*
   - *Lakota*
   - *Crow*
   - *Teton*
   - *Hopi*
   - *Inuit*

INTEGRATED CIVICS

A: Geography

CD 2
Track 16

88. **Name <u>one</u> of the two longest rivers in the United States.**
   - *Missouri (River)*
   - *Mississippi (River)*

89. **What ocean is on the West Coast of the United States?**
   - *Pacific (Ocean)*

90. **What ocean is on the East Coast of the United States?**
   - *Atlantic (Ocean)*

91. Name <u>one</u> U.S. territory.
- *Puerto Rico*
- *U.S. Virgin Islands*
- *American Samoa*
- *Northern Mariana Islands*
- *Guam*

92. Name <u>one</u> state that borders Canada.
- *Maine*
- *New Hampshire*
- *Vermont*
- *New York*
- *Pennsylvania*
- *Ohio*
- *Michigan*
- *Minnesota*
- *North Dakota*
- *Montana*
- *Idaho*
- *Washington*
- *Alaska*

93. Name <u>one</u> state that borders Mexico.
- *California*
- *Arizona*
- *New Mexico*
- *Texas*

94. What is the capital of the United States?*
- *Washington, D.C.*

95. Where is the Statue of Liberty?*
- *New York (Harbor)*
- *Liberty Island*
- *New Jersey*
- *near New York City*
- *on the Hudson (River)*

B: Symbols

96. Why does the flag have 13 stripes?
- *because there were 13 original colonies*
- *because the stripes represent the original colonies*

CD 2
Track 17

97. Why does the flag have 50 stars?*
- *because there is one star for each state*
- *because each star represents a state*
- *because there are 50 states*

98. What is the name of the national anthem?
- *The Star-Spangled Banner*

C: Holidays

99. When do we celebrate Independence Day?*
- *July 4*

100. Name <u>two</u> national U.S. holidays.
- *New Year's Day*
- *Martin Luther King, Jr. Day*
- *Presidents' Day*
- *Memorial Day*
- *Independence Day*
- *Labor Day*
- *Columbus Day*
- *Veterans Day*
- *Thanksgiving*
- *Christmas*

USCIS N-400 Form

Department of Homeland Security
U.S Citizenship and Immigration Services

OMB No. 1615-0052

N-400 Application for Naturalization

Print clearly or type your answers using CAPITAL letters. Failure to print clearly may delay your application. Use black ink.

Part 1. Your Name. *(The person applying for naturalization.)*

A. Your current legal name.

Family Name *(Last Name)*

[ ]

Given Name *(First Name)*

[ ]

Full Middle Name *(If applicable)*

[ ]

B. Your name **exactly** as it appears on your Permanent Resident Card.

Family Name *(Last Name)*

[ ]

Given Name *(First Name)*

[ ]

Full Middle Name *(If applicable)*

[ ]

C. If you have ever used other names, provide them below.

Family Name *(Last Name)*	Given Name *(First Name)*	Middle Name

D. Name change *(optional)*

Please read the Instructions before you decide whether to change your name.

1. Would you like to legally change your name? [ ] Yes [ ] No

2. If "Yes," print the new name you would like to use. Do not use initials or abbreviations when writing your new name.

Family Name *(Last Name)*

[ ]

Given Name *(First Name)*

[ ]

Full Middle Name

[ ]

Write your USCIS "A"- number here:
A

For USCIS Use Only

Bar Code	Date Stamp

Remarks

Action Block

Part 2. Information about your eligibility. *(Check only one.)*

I am at least 18 years old **AND**

A. [ ] I have been a Lawful Permanent Resident of the United States for at least five years.

B. [ ] I have been a Lawful Permanent Resident of the United States for at least three years, **and** I have been married to and living with the same U.S. citizen for the last three years, **and** my spouse has been a U.S. citizen for the last three years.

C. [ ] I am applying on the basis of qualifying military service.

D. [ ] Other *(Please explain)* _____

Write your USCIS "A"- number here:
A

A. U.S. Social Security Number

B. Date of Birth *(mm/dd/yyyy)*

C. Date You Became a Permanent Resident *(mm/dd/yyyy)*

D. Country of Birth

E. Country of Nationality

F. Are either of your parents U.S. citizens? *(If yes, see instructions.)* ☐ Yes ☐ No

G. What is your current marital status? ☐ Single, Never Married ☐ Married ☐ Divorced ☐ Widowed

☐ Marriage Annulled or Other *(Explain)* _____

H. Are you requesting a waiver of the English and/or U.S. History and Government requirements based on a disability or impairment and attaching a Form N-648 with your application? ☐ Yes ☐ No

I. Are you requesting an accommodation to the naturalization process because of a disability or impairment? *(See Instructions for some examples of accommodations.)* ☐ Yes ☐ No

If you answered "Yes," check the box below that applies:

☐ I am deaf or hearing impaired and need a sign language interpreter who uses the following language: _____

☐ I use a wheelchair.

☐ I am blind or sight impaired.

☐ I will need another type of accommodation. Please explain: _____

_____

_____

A. Home Address - Street Number and Name *(Do **not** write a P.O. Box in this space.)*

Apartment Number

City	County	State	ZIP Code	Country

B. Care of

Mailing Address - Street Number and Name *(If different from home address)*

Apartment Number

City	State	ZIP Code	Country

C. Daytime Phone Number *(If any)*

( )

Evening Phone Number *(If any)*

( )

E-mail Address *(If any)*

Part 5. Information for criminal records search.

NOTE: The categories below are those required by the FBI. See Instructions for more information.

A. Gender

☐ Male ☐ Female

B. Height

| Feet | Inches |

C. Weight

| Pounds |

D. Are you Hispanic or Latino? ☐ Yes ☐ No

E. Race *(Select one or more.)*

☐ White ☐ Asian ☐ Black or African American ☐ American Indian or Alaskan Native ☐ Native Hawaiian or Other Pacific Islander

F. Hair color

☐ Black ☐ Brown ☐ Blonde ☐ Gray ☐ White ☐ Red ☐ Sandy ☐ Bald (No Hair)

G. Eye color

☐ Brown ☐ Blue ☐ Green ☐ Hazel ☐ Gray ☐ Black ☐ Pink ☐ Maroon ☐ Other

Part 6. Information about your residence and employment.

A. Where have you lived during the last five years? Begin with where you live now and then list every place you lived for the last five years. If you need more space, use a separate sheet(s) of paper.

Street Number and Name, Apartment Number, City, State, Zip Code and Country	Dates *(mm/dd/yyyy)*	
	From	To
Current Home Address - Same as Part 4.A		Present

B. Where have you worked (or, if you were a student, what schools did you attend) during the last five years? Include military service. Begin with your current or latest employer and then list every place you have worked or studied for the last five years. If you need more space, use a separate sheet of paper.

Employer or School Name	Employer or School Address *(Street, City and State)*	Dates *(mm/dd/yyyy)*		Your Occupation
		From	To	

Form N-400 (Rev. 10/15/07) Y Page 3

Part 7. Time outside the United States.
(Including Trips to Canada, Mexico and the Caribbean Islands)

Write your USCIS "A"- number here:
A

A. How many total days did you spend outside of the United States during the past five years? [ ] days

B. How many trips of 24 hours or more have you taken outside of the United States during the past five years? [ ] trips

C. List below all the trips of 24 hours or more that you have taken outside of the United States since becoming a Lawful Permanent Resident. Begin with your most recent trip. If you need more space, use a separate sheet(s) of paper.

Date You Left the United States (mm/dd/yyyy)	Date You Returned to the United States (mm/dd/yyyy)	Did Trip Last Six Months or More?	Countries to Which You Traveled	Total Days Out of the United States
		[ ] Yes [ ] No		
		[ ] Yes [ ] No		
		[ ] Yes [ ] No		
		[ ] Yes [ ] No		
		[ ] Yes [ ] No		
		[ ] Yes [ ] No		
		[ ] Yes [ ] No		
		[ ] Yes [ ] No		
		[ ] Yes [ ] No		
		[ ] Yes [ ] No		

Part 8. Information about your marital history.

A. How many times have you been married (including annulled marriages)? [ ] If you have **never** been married, go to Part 9.

B. If you are now married, give the following information about your spouse:

1. Spouse's Family Name *(Last Name)*   Given Name *(First Name)*   Full Middle Name *(If applicable)*

2. Date of Birth *(mm/dd/yyyy)*   **3.** Date of Marriage *(mm/dd/yyyy)*   **4.** Spouse's U.S. Social Security #

5. Home Address - Street Number and Name   Apartment Number

City   State   Zip Code

C. Is your spouse a U.S. citizen? ☐ Yes ☐ No

D. If your spouse is a U.S. citizen, give the following information:

1. When did your spouse become a U.S. citizen? ☐ At Birth ☐ Other

If "Other," give the following information:

2. Date your spouse became a U.S. citizen

3. Place your spouse became a U.S. citizen *(Please see Instructions.)*

City and State

E. If your spouse is **not** a U.S. citizen, give the following information :

1. Spouse's Country of Citizenship

2. Spouse's USCIS "A"- Number *(If applicable)*
A

3. Spouse's Immigration Status
☐ Lawful Permanent Resident ☐ Other

F. If you were married before, provide the following information about your prior spouse. If you have more than one previous marriage, use a separate sheet(s) of paper to provide the information requested in Questions 1-5 below.

1. Prior Spouse's Family Name *(Last Name)*   Given Name *(First Name)*   Full Middle Name *(If applicable)*

2. Prior Spouse's Immigration Status
☐ U.S. Citizen
☐ Lawful Permanent Resident
☐ Other

3. Date of Marriage *(mm/dd/yyyy)*

4. Date Marriage Ended *(mm/dd/yyyy)*

5. How Marriage Ended
☐ Divorce ☐ Spouse Died ☐ Other

G. How many times has your current spouse been married (including annulled marriages)?

If your spouse has **ever** been married before, give the following information about **your spouse's** prior marriage.
If your spouse has more than one previous marriage, use a separate sheet(s) of paper to provide the information requested in Questions 1 - 5 below.

1. Prior Spouse's Family Name *(Last Name)*   Given Name *(First Name)*   Full Middle Name *(If applicable)*

2. Prior Spouse's Immigration Status
☐ U.S. Citizen
☐ Lawful Permanent Resident
☐ Other

3. Date of Marriage *(mm/dd/yyyy)*

4. Date Marriage Ended *(mm/dd/yyyy)*

5. How Marriage Ended
☐ Divorce ☐ Spouse Died ☐ Other

Form N-400 (Rev. 10/15/07) Y Page 5

A. How many sons and daughters have you had? For more information on which sons and daughters you should include and how to complete this section, see the Instructions.

B. Provide the following information about all of your sons and daughters. If you need more space, use a separate sheet(s) of paper.

Full Name of Son or Daughter	Date of Birth (mm/dd/yyyy)	USCIS "A"- number (if child has one)	Country of Birth	Current Address (Street, City, State and Country)
		A		
		A		
		A		
		A		
		A		
		A		
		A		
		A		

Add Children		Go to continuation page

Part 10. Additional questions.

Please answer Questions 1 through 14. If you answer "Yes" to any of these questions, include a written explanation with this form. Your written explanation should (1) explain why your answer was "Yes" and (2) provide any additional information that helps to explain your answer.

A. General Questions.

1. Have you **ever** claimed to be a U.S. citizen *(in writing or any other way)*? ☐ Yes ☐ No

2. Have you **ever** registered to vote in any Federal, state or local election in the United States? ☐ Yes ☐ No

3. Have you **ever** voted in any Federal, state or local election in the United States? ☐ Yes ☐ No

4. Since becoming a Lawful Permanent Resident, have you **ever** failed to file a required Federal state or local tax return? ☐ Yes ☐ No

5. Do you owe any Federal, state or local taxes that are overdue? ☐ Yes ☐ No

6. Do you have any title of nobility in any foreign country? ☐ Yes ☐ No

7. Have you ever been declared legally incompetent or been confined to a mental institution within the last five years? ☐ Yes ☐ No

Write your USCIS "A"- number here:
A

B. Affiliations.

8. a Have you **ever** been a member of or associated with any organization, association, fund foundation, party, club, society or similar group in the United States or in any other place? ☐ Yes ☐ No

  b. If you answered "Yes," list the name of each group below. If you need more space, attach the names of the other group(s) on a separate sheet(s) of paper.

Name of Group	Name of Group
1.	6.
2.	7.
3.	8.
4.	9.
5.	10.

9. Have you **ever** been a member of or in any way associated *(either directly or indirectly)* with:

  a. The Communist Party? ☐ Yes ☐ No

  b. Any other totalitarian party? ☐ Yes ☐ No

  c. A terrorist organization? ☐ Yes ☐ No

10. Have you **ever** advocated *(either directly or indirectly)* the overthrow of any government by force or violence? ☐ Yes ☐ No

11. Have you **ever** persecuted *(either directly or indirectly)* any person because of race, religion, national origin, membership in a particular social group or political opinion? ☐ Yes ☐ No

12. Between March 23, 1933 and May 8, 1945, did you work for or associate in any way *(either directly or indirectly)* with:

  a. The Nazi government of Germany? ☐ Yes ☐ No

  b. Any government in any area (1) occupied by, (2) allied with, or (3) established with the help of the Nazi government of Germany? ☐ Yes ☐ No

  c. Any German, Nazi, or S.S. military unit, paramilitary unit, self-defense unit, vigilante unit, citizen unit, police unit, government agency or office, extermination camp, concentration camp, prisoner of war camp, prison, labor camp or transit camp? ☐ Yes ☐ No

C. Continuous Residence.

Since becoming a Lawful Permanent Resident of the United States:

13. Have you **ever** called yourself a "nonresident" on a Federal, state or local tax return? ☐ Yes ☐ No

14. Have you **ever** failed to file a Federal, state or local tax return because you considered yourself to be a "nonresident"? ☐ Yes ☐ No

D. Good Moral Character.

For the purposes of this application, you must answer "Yes" to the following questions, if applicable, even if your records were sealed or otherwise cleared or if anyone, including a judge, law enforcement officer or attorney, told you that you no longer have a record.

15. Have you **ever** committed a crime or offense for which you were **not** arrested?   ☐ Yes   ☐ No

16. Have you **ever** been arrested, cited or detained by any law enforcement officer (including USCIS or former INS and military officers) for any reason?   ☐ Yes   ☐ No

17. Have you **ever** been charged with committing any crime or offense?   ☐ Yes   ☐ No

18. Have you **ever** been convicted of a crime or offense?   ☐ Yes   ☐ No

19. Have you **ever** been placed in an alternative sentencing or a rehabilitative program (for example: diversion, deferred prosecution, withheld adjudication, deferred adjudication)?   ☐ Yes   ☐ No

20. Have you **ever** received a suspended sentence, been placed on probation or been paroled?   ☐ Yes   ☐ No

21. Have you **ever** been in jail or prison?   ☐ Yes   ☐ No

If you answered "Yes" to any of Questions 15 through 21, complete the following table. If you need more space, use a separate sheet(s) of paper to give the same information.

Why were you arrested, cited, detained or charged?	Date arrested, cited, detained or charged? *(mm/dd/yyyy)*	Where were you arrested, cited, detained or charged? *(City, State, Country)*	Outcome or disposition of the arrest, citation, detention or charge *(No charges filed, charges dismissed, jail, probation, etc.)*
			.

Answer Questions 22 through 33. If you answer "Yes" to any of these questions, attach (1) your written explanation why your answer was "Yes" and (2) any additional information or documentation that helps explain your answer.

22. Have you **ever**:

    a. Been a habitual drunkard?   ☐ Yes   ☐ No

    b. Been a prostitute, or procured anyone for prostitution?   ☐ Yes   ☐ No

    c. Sold or smuggled controlled substances, illegal drugs or narcotics?   ☐ Yes   ☐ No

    d. Been married to more than one person at the same time?   ☐ Yes   ☐ No

    e. Helped anyone enter or try to enter the United States illegally?   ☐ Yes   ☐ No

    f. Gambled illegally or received income from illegal gambling?   ☐ Yes   ☐ No

    g. Failed to support your dependents or to pay alimony?   ☐ Yes   ☐ No

23. Have you **ever** given false or misleading information to any U.S. government official while applying for any immigration benefit or to prevent deportation, exclusion or removal?   ☐ Yes   ☐ No

24. Have you **ever** lied to any U.S. government official to gain entry or admission into the United States?   ☐ Yes   ☐ No

Write your USCIS "A"- number here:
A

E. Removal, Exclusion and Deportation Proceedings.

25. Are removal, exclusion, rescission or deportation proceedings pending against you? ☐ Yes ☐ No

26. Have you **ever** been removed, excluded or deported from the United States? ☐ Yes ☐ No

27. Have you **ever** been ordered to be removed, excluded or deported from the United States? ☐ Yes ☐ No

28. Have you **ever** applied for any kind of relief from removal, exclusion or deportation? ☐ Yes ☐ No

F. Military Service.

29. Have you **ever** served in the U.S. Armed Forces? ☐ Yes ☐ No

30. Have you **ever** left the United States to avoid being drafted into the U.S. Armed Forces? ☐ Yes ☐ No

31. Have you **ever** applied for any kind of exemption from military service in the U.S. Armed Forces? ☐ Yes ☐ No

32. Have you **ever** deserted from the U.S. Armed Forces? ☐ Yes ☐ No

G. Selective Service Registration.

33. Are you a male who lived in the United States at any time between your 18th and 26th birthdays in any status except as a lawful nonimmigrant? ☐ Yes ☐ No

   If you answered "NO," go on to question 34.

   If you answered "YES," provide the information below.

   If you answered "YES," but you did not register with the Selective Service System and are still under 26 years of age, you must register before you apply for naturalization, so that you can complete the information below:

   Date Registered (mm/dd/yyyy) [   ]   Selective Service Number [   ]

   If you answered "YES," but you did not register with the Selective Service and you are now 26 years old or older, attach a statement explaining why you did not register.

H. Oath Requirements. *(See Part 14 for the Text of the Oath.)*

Answer Questions 34 through 39. If you answer "No" to any of these questions, attach (1) your written explanation why the answer was "No" and (2) any additional information or documentation that helps to explain your answer.

34. Do you support the Constitution and form of government of the United States? ☐ Yes ☐ No

35. Do you understand the full Oath of Allegiance to the United States? ☐ Yes ☐ No

36. Are you willing to take the full Oath of Allegiance to the United States? ☐ Yes ☐ No

37. If the law requires it, are you willing to bear arms on behalf of the United States? ☐ Yes ☐ No

38. If the law requires it, are you willing to perform noncombatant services in the U.S. Armed Forces? ☐ Yes ☐ No

39. If the law requires it, are you willing to perform work of national importance under civilian direction? ☐ Yes ☐ No

Part 11. Your signature.

I certify, under penalty of perjury under the laws of the United States of America, that this application, and the evidence submitted with it, are all true and correct. I authorize the release of any information that the USCIS needs to determine my eligibility for naturalization.

Your Signature

Date (mm/dd/yyyy)

Part 12. Signature of person who prepared this application for you. *(If applicable.)*

I declare under penalty of perjury that I prepared this application at the request of the above person. The answers provided are based on information of which I have personal knowledge and/or were provided to me by the above named person in response to the *exact question*, contained on this form.

Preparer's Printed Name

Preparer's Signature

Date (mm/dd/yyyy)

Preparer's Firm or Organization Name (If applicable)

Preparer's Daytime Phone Number

Preparer's Address - Street Number and Name

City

State

Zip Code

NOTE: Do not complete Parts 13 and 14 until a USCIS Officer instructs you to do so.

Part 13. Signature at interview.

I swear (affirm) and certify under penalty of perjury under the laws of the United States of America that I know that the contents of this application for naturalization subscribed by me, including corrections numbered 1 through _____ and the evidence submitted by me numbered pages 1 through _____ , are true and correct to the best of my knowledge and belief.

Subscribed to and sworn to (affirmed) before me

Officer's Printed Name or Stamp

Date (mm/dd/yyyy)

Complete Signature of Applicant

Officer's Signature

Part 14. Oath of Allegiance.

If your application is approved, you will be scheduled for a public oath ceremony at which time you will be required to take the following oath of allegiance immediately prior to becoming a naturalized citizen. By signing, you acknowledge your willingness and ability to take this oath:

I hereby declare, on oath, that I absolutely and entirely renounce and abjure all allegiance and fidelity to any foreign prince, potentate, state, or sovereignty, of whom or which I have heretofore been a subject or citizen;

that I will support and defend the Constitution and laws of the United States of America against all enemies, foreign and domestic;

that I will bear true faith and allegiance to the same;

that I will bear arms on behalf of the United States when required by the law;

that I will perform noncombatant service in the Armed Forces of the United States when required by the law;

that I will perform work of national importance under civilian direction when required by the law; and

that I take this obligation freely, without any mental reservation or purpose of evasion; so help me God.

Printed Name of Applicant

Complete Signature of Applicant

Form N-400 (Rev. 10/15/07) Y Page 10

World Map

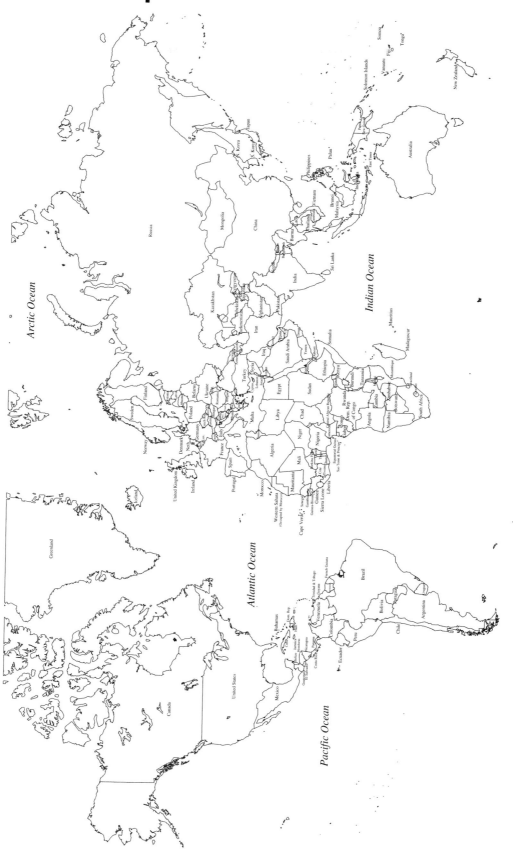

U.S. Map

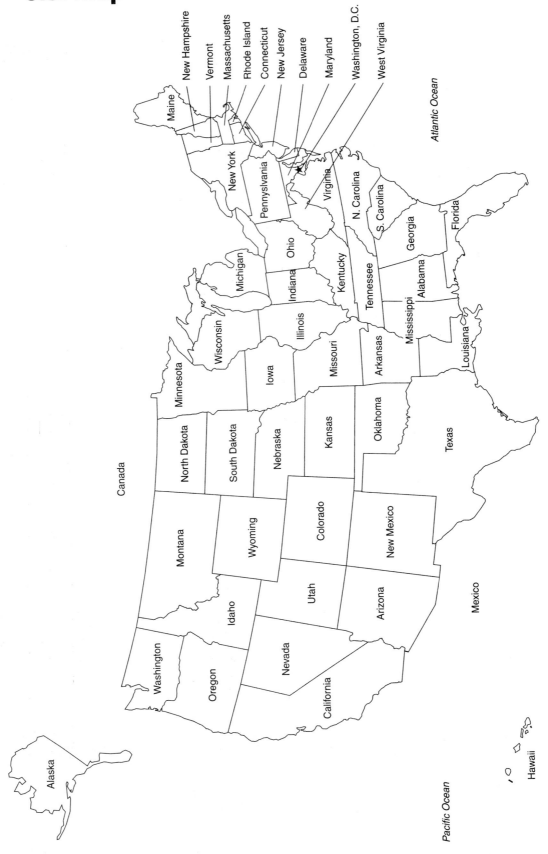

Appendix C

Answer Key

Unit 1

3. After You Read

A.

1. Columbus
2. Columbus; Pilgrims
3. Pilgrims
4. Columbus
5. Pilgrims
6. Pilgrims

B.

1. India
2. landed
3. Indians
4. colony
5. died
6. missions
7. Pilgrims
8. religious freedom
9. Mayflower
10. Thanksgiving
11. Africans
12. slaves

7. Take the Test

A

1. b
2. d
3. b
4. d
5. b
6. d
7. b

C.

1. I live in the United States of America.
2. The American Indians helped the Pilgrims.
3. When do we celebrate Thanksgiving?
4. Thanksgiving Day is the fourth Thursday in November.

Game # 1

1. He was an explorer and trader. / He was an explorer looking for a new way to India.
2. India

3. the *Niña*, the *Pinta*, and the *Santa María*

4. on an island in the Caribbean Sea / on San Salvador Island

5. Columbus named the Native Americans *indios,* or Indians.

6. spices, silk, and gold

7. slaves

8. the New World

9. The Native Americans (the American Indians)

10. Cherokee, Navajo, Sioux, Chippewa, Choctaw, Pueblo, Apache, Iroquois, Creek, Blackfeet, Seminole, Cheyenne, Arawak, Shawnee, Mohegan, Huron, Oneida, Lakota, Crow, Teton, Hopi, Inuit

11. for freedom, for political liberty, for religious freedom, for economic opportunity, to practice their religion, to escape persecution

12. 1620

13. They sailed on the ship called the *Mayflower.*

14. England (Great Britain)

15. for religious freedom

16. Virginia

17. The Mayflower landed at Plymouth, Massachusetts (Plymouth Rock).

18. Native Americans (American Indians)

19. 1621

20. turkey, stuffing, corn, and pumpkin pie

21. on the fourth Thursday in November

Unit 2

3. After You Read

A.

1. True	4. True
2. False	5. True
3. False	6. True

B.

1. taxed	5. Revolutionary War	9. Declaration of Independence
2. angry	6. 1783	10. equal
3. free	7. won	11. right
4. tea	8. Washington	12. July 4, 1776

7. Take the Test

A.

1. b	**5.** d
2. d	**6.** c
3. b	**7.** b
4. d	**8.** c

C.

1. George Washington is the "Father of Our Country."
2. July 4 is Independence Day.
3. George Washington was the first president.
4. There were thirteen (13) colonies.

Game # 2

1. George III
2. tea, stamps, and sugar
3. The colonists thought the taxes were unfair. / The colonists were angry.
4. Patrick Henry
5. five colonists in the city of Boston / Crispus Attucks
6. Colonists threw 90,000 pounds of tea into the water.
7. The colonists wanted independence from England (Great Britain).
8. 1775
9. England (Great Britain) and the American colonists
10. George Washington
11. 1783
12. the United States / the thirteen (13) colonies
13. George Washington
14. All men are created equal.
15. Thomas Jefferson
16. July 4, 1776
17. life, liberty, and the pursuit of happiness
18. Independence Day
19. George Washington

Unit 3

3. After You Read

A.

1. True
2. False
3. True
4. True
5. False
6. True

B.

1. Constitution
2. Philadelphia
3. supreme
4. government
5. Bill of Rights
6. amendments
7. twenty-seven
8. vote
9. 18
10. Twenty-Sixth
11. freedom of speech
12. religion
13. press
14. assembly
15. noncitizens

7. Take the Test

A.

1. a
2. b
3. c
4. b
5. b
6. b
7. d
8. c

C.

1. We have freedom of speech in the United States.
2. A citizen has the right to vote.
3. The Constitution is the supreme law of the land.
4. The Bill of Rights is the first ten amendments.

Game # 3

1. the Constitution
2. sets up the government / defines the government / protects the basic rights of Americans
3. 1787
4. the Preamble
5. *We the People*
6. an amendment
7. twenty-seven (27)
8. legislative (Congress), executive (president), and judicial (courts)
9. pass laws / collect taxes / print money / organize an army / declare war / make treaties
10. a representative democracy (a republic)

11. checks and balances / separation of powers
12. the Thirteenth Amendment
13. the Nineteenth Amendment
14. citizens and noncitizens
15. freedom of speech / freedom of the press / freedom of religion / the right to assemble (hold a meeting) / the right to ask for a change of government
16. The rights of everyone living in the United States, both citizens and noncitizens include: freedom of expression / freedom of speech / freedom of assembly / freedom of worship / freedom to petition the government / the right to bear arms
17. the right to vote
18. Fifteenth Amendment / Nineteenth Amendment / Twenty-Fourth Amendment / Twenty-Sixth Amendment
19. Everyone must follow the law. / Leaders must obey the law. / Government must obey the law. / No one is above the law.

Unit 4

3. After You Read

A.

1. Atlantic Ocean
2. Canada
3. Mississippi River / Missouri River
4. Mexico
5. Pacific Ocean
6. The United States

B.

1. 1861
2. South (Confederacy)
3. Abraham Lincoln
4. Emancipation Proclamation

C.

1. expanded
2. Louisiana
3. Mississippi River
4. immigrants
5. Africa
6. slaves
7. free
8. North
9. South
10. slavery
11. Civil
12. won
13. Emancipation Proclamation
14. Thirteenth

⭐ 7. Take the Test

A.

1. c   5. d
2. a   6. d
3. c   7. a
4. b   8. d

C.

1. Lincoln's birthday is February 12.
2. The Civil War was between the North and the South.
3. Presidents' Day is in February.
4. Canada is north of the United States.
5. Mexico is south of the United States.

Game # 4

1. west
2. the Louisiana Territory
3. immigrants
4. Missouri
5. Slaves
6. Africans
7. slaves
8. free
9. North
10. Underground
11. president
12. 1861
13. Emancipation Proclamation
14. freed
15. 600,000
16. 1865
17. assassinated
18. Thirteenth
19. rights
20. slavery

Unit 5

3. After You Read

A.
1. True
2. False
3. True
4. True
5. False
6. True
7. True

B.
1. shorter
2. England
3. Russia
4. 1918
5. Franklin Delano Roosevelt
6. 1939
7. bombs
8. world problems
9. Dr. Martin Luther King, Jr.
10. speech
11. Communism
12. terrorists

7. Take the Test

A.
1. c
2. d
3. b
4. b
5. a
6. d
7. a
8. b

C.
1. We are all free in the United States.
2. Columbus Day is in October.
3. There are fifty (50) states.
4. Many people died on September 11, 2001.

Game # 5
1. shorter work days, rest periods, better pay, safer jobs
2. fought for women's rights / fought for civil rights
3. 1914
4. Woodrow Wilson
5. The United States did not want to be involved in the problems of other countries.
6. 1918
7. England, France, Russia, and the United States
8. People lost their jobs, their savings, and their homes. Many people were hungry. People organized and demanded help from the government.
9. Franklin Delano Roosevelt

10. People built roads, dams, post offices, and theaters. Some small businesses got government loans. Congress passed the Social Security Act and welfare programs.
11. 1939
12. Dwight D. Eisenhower
13. England, France, Russia, and the United States
14. Germany, Italy, and Japan
15. the Allies (England, France, Russia, and the United States)
16. More than ten million Jews, Catholics, homosexuals, and gypsies were killed by Hitler and the Nazis.
17. At the UN, representatives from different countries discuss and try to resolve world problems.
18. 1973
19. He fought for civil rights. / He worked for the equality of all Americans.
20. Civil Rights movement
21. Terrorists attacked the United States.

Unit 6

After You Read

A.

1. True   4. True
2. False   5. False
3. True   6. False

B.

1. The Pledge of Allegiance
2. "The Star-Spangled Banner"
3. "The Star-Spangled Banner"
4. The Pledge of Allegiance
5. The Pledge of Allegiance
6. The Pledge of Allegiance and "The Star-Spangled Banner"

C.

1. d
2. a
3. b
4. c

D.

1. stripes
2. stars
3. colonies
4. states

5. "The Star-Spangled Banner"
6. anthem
7. Independence Day
8. Pledge

9. republic
10. justice
11. Statue

 7. Take the Test

A.

1. b
2. b
3. a
4. b

5. a
6. c
7. a
8. d

C.

1. The American flag is red, white, and blue.
2. The United States has fifty (50) states.
3. Memorial Day is the last Monday in May.
4. The United States flag has thirteen (13) stripes.
5. Flag Day is in June.

Game # 6

1. fifty (50)
2. because there is one star for each state / because each star represents a state / because there are fifty states
3. because there were 13 original colonies / because the stripes represent the original colonies
4. red, white, and blue
5. July 4
6. the third Monday in January
7. the third Monday in February
8. November 11
9. "The Star-Spangled Banner"
10. Francis Scott Key
11. liberty and freedom
12. New York Harbor / Liberty Island / New Jersey / near New York City / on the Hudson River
13. "The New Colossus" by Emma Lazarus
14. New Year's Day / Martin Luther King, Jr. Day / Presidents' Day / Memorial Day / Independence Day / Labor Day / Columbus Day / Veterans Day / Thanksgiving / Christmas
15. heart

16. *I pledge allegiance to the Flag of the United States of America, and to the Republic for which it stands, one Nation under God, indivisible, with Liberty and Justice for all.*

17. on holidays and at some public ceremonies

18. Alaska and Hawaii

Unit 7

3. After You Read

B.

1. House of Representatives
2. Senate
3. House of Representatives and Senate
4. House of Representatives and Senate
5. Senate

C.

1. Congress
2. laws
3. Senate
4. House of Representatives
5. president
6. 100
7. vice president
8. 435
9. Speaker
10. 18
11. Democratic
12. Republican

7. Take the Test

A.

1. c
2. a
3. b
4. d
5. b
6. c
7. d
8. b

C.

1. The Congress meets in the Capitol Building.
2. There are two (2) senators from each state.
3. The Congress makes the laws in the United States.
4. Washington, D.C. is the capital of the United States.
5. There are one hundred (100) senators.
6. Citizens elect their senators and representatives.

Game # 7

1. Congress
2. the House of Representatives and the Senate
3. in the Capitol Building in Washington, D.C.

4. Congress makes federal laws.

5. They are elected by the people.

6. 100

7. Each state has two senators.

8. six (6) years

9. 30 years old

10. all the people of the state

11. 435

12. 25 years old

13. two years

14. because they have a bigger population

15. the vice president

16. the Speaker of the House

17. yes

18. declare war, make laws, collect taxes, borrow money, control immigration, set up a judicial system, set up a postal system

19. legislative (Congress), executive (president), and judicial (courts)

20. 18 years old

21. Answers will vary by state.

22. Answers will vary by state.

Unit 8

3. After You Read

B.

1. the executive branch

2. the judicial branch

3. the executive branch

4. the judicial branch and the executive branch

5. the judicial branch

C.

1. executive

2. president

3. four

4. terms

5. November

6. electoral college

7. cabinet

8. vice president

9. Speaker

10. Supreme Court

11. explains

12. nine

7. Take the Test

A.

1. a
2. c
3. a and c
4. d

5. a
6. b
7. c
8. a

C.

1. The president lives in the White House.
2. Washington, D.C., is the capital of the United States.
3. The president is elected in November.
4. Alaska is the largest state.
5. I want to live in the United States.

Game # 8

1. three (3) branches
2. legislative (Congress), executive (president), judicial (courts)
3. the legislative branch (Congress)
4. the judicial branch (courts)
5. the executive branch (president)
6. the president
7. November
8. The president must be a natural-born citizen of the United States, must be at least 35 years old, and must have lived in the United States for fourteen years.
9. four (4) years
10. the president
11. the president
12. advises the president
13. the vice president
14. Barack Obama
15. 1600 Pennsylvania Avenue NW, Washington, D.C.
16. two (2)
17. Secretary of Agriculture / Secretary of Commerce / Secretary of Defense / Secretary of Education / Secretary of Energy / Secretary of Health and Human Services / Secretary of Homeland Security / Secretary of Housing and Urban Development / Secretary of Interior / Secretary of State / Secretary of Transportation / Secretary of Treasury / Secretary of Veterans' Affairs / Secretary of Labor / Attorney General
18. the Supreme Court
19. nine (9)
20. appointed by the president and approved by Congress
21. John Roberts (John G. Roberts, Jr.)

Unit 9

3. After You Read

A.

1. Federal
2. State
3. Federal and State
4. Federal and State
5. Federal

B.

1. constitution
2. legislative
3. judicial
4. governor
5. Answers will vary depending on state.
6. Answers will vary depending on state.
7. education
8. public protection
9. mayor
10. Answers will vary depending on city.
11. city council
12. trash
13. libraries

7. Take The Test

A.

1. b
2. b
3. a
4. Answers will vary by state.
5. Answers will vary by community.
6. Answers will vary by state.
7. a
8. Answers will vary by state.

C.

1. I live in _____ , _____ .
   (city)   (state)
2. The vice president lives in Washington, D.C.
3. The mayor of this city is _____ .
4. The governor of this state is _____ .
5. Delaware was the first state in this country.
6. Why did you come to the United States?

Game # 9

1. Answers will vary by state.
2. Answers will vary by state.
3. Answers will vary by state.
4. Answers will vary by state.
5. yes
6. yes
7. legislative, executive, judicial

8. legislative

9. The governor enforces state laws.

10. Answers will vary by state.

11. from taxes

12. States provide services in schooling and education, public protection (police) and safety (fire), jails, welfare, roads, public health, and regulation of businesses. / States make laws about work, school, property, and marriage.

13. Answers will vary by state.

14. Answers will vary by state.

15. Answers will vary by state.

16. the United States of America

17. Answers will vary.

18. Answers will vary.

Unit 10

3. After You Read

A.

1. 18
2. Lawful
3. write
4. register
5. history
6. questions
7. N-400
8. moral
9. taxes
10. April 15
11. obey
12. vote
13. opinion

7. Take the Test

A.

1. c
2. a
3. b
4. a and b
5. b
6. c
7. b
8. speak

C.

1. What colors are in the American flag?
2. Do you have a one-dollar bill?
3. California has the most people of any state.
4. Labor Day is in September.
5. How long have you lived here?

Audio Script

Unit 1, Take the Test, Section 7A. Multiple Choice Questions.
Listen to the questions. Circle the correct answers.

1. Who lived in America before the Europeans arrived?
2. Why did colonists come to America?
3. Who helped the Pilgrims in America?
4. What was the name of the Pilgrims' ship?
5. What holiday was celebrated for the first time by the American colonists?
6. Name two American Indian (Native American) tribes in the United States.
7. Africans were brought to America and sold as _____ .

Unit 1, Take the Test, Section 7B.
Now, listen again and check your answers.

1. Who lived in America before the Europeans arrived?
   Answer: b. the American Indians (Native Americans)
2. Why did colonists come to America?
   Answer: d. for religious freedom and economic opportunity
3. Who helped the Pilgrims in America?
   Answer: b. the Native Americans (American Indians)
4. What was the name of the Pilgrims' ship?
   Answer: d. the *Mayflower*
5. What holiday was celebrated for the first time by the American colonists?
   Answer: b. Thanksgiving
6. Name two American Indian (Native American) tribes in the United States.
   Answer: d. the Iroquois and the Algonquin
7. Africans were brought to America and sold as _____ .
   Answer: b. slaves

Unit 1, Take the Test, Section 7C. Writing Vocabulary Dictation
Listen to each sentence. Then, listen again and write what you hear.

1. I live in the United States of America.
2. The American Indians helped the Pilgrims.
3. When do we celebrate Thanksgiving?
4. Thanksgiving Day is the fourth Thursday in November.

CD 1
Track 4

Unit 2, Take the Test, Section 7A. Multiple Choice Questions
Listen to the questions. Circle the correct answers.

1. Who was the main writer of the Declaration of Independence?
2. When was the Declaration of Independence adopted?
3. What did the Declaration of Independence say?
4. What is another name for England?
5. Why did the colonists fight the British?
6. Who said, "Give me liberty or give me death!"?
7. Which president is called the "Father of Our Country"?
8. What is another name for the American Revolution?

CD 1
Track 5

Unit 2, Take the Test, Section 7B.
Now, listen again and check your answers.

1. Who was the main writer of the Declaration of Independence?
   Answer: b. Thomas Jefferson
2. When was the Declaration of Independence adopted?
   Answer: d. July 4, 1776
3. What did the Declaration of Independence say?
   Answer: b. The United States was free from Great Britain.
4. What is another name for England?
   Answer: d. Great Britain
5. Why did the colonists fight the British?
   Answer: d. because of high taxes, the British army stayed in their homes, and they didn't have self-government
6. Who said, "Give me liberty or give me death!"?
   Answer: c. Patrick Henry
7. Which president is called the "Father of Our Country"?
   Answer: b. George Washington
8. What is another name for the American Revolution?
   Answer: c. Revolutionary War

CD 1
Track 6

Unit 2, Take the Test, Section 7C. Writing Vocabulary Dictation
Listen to each sentence. Then, listen again and write what you hear.

1. George Washington is the "Father of Our Country."
2. July 4 is Independence Day.
3. George Washington was the first president.
4. There were thirteen colonies.

Unit 3, Take the Test, Section 7A. Multiple Choice Questions.

Listen to the questions. Circle the correct answers.

1. What is the supreme law of the United States?
2. What happened at the Constitutional Convention of 1787?
3. What is the introduction to the Constitution called?
4. What do we call a change to the Constitution?
5. What is one power of the federal government?
6. Who wrote the Federalist Papers?
7. What is the economic system of the United States?
8. What is one thing Benjamin Franklin is famous for?

Unit 3, Take the Test, Section 7B.

Now, listen again and check your answers.

1. What is the supreme law of the United States?
   Answer: a. the Constitution
2. What happened at the Constitutional Convention of 1787?
   Answer: b. The Constitution was written.
3. What is the introduction to the Constitution called?
   Answer: c. the Preamble
4. What do we call a change to the Constitution?
   Answer: b. an amendment
5. What is one power of the federal government?
   Answer: b. to print money
6. Who wrote the Federalist Papers?
   Answer: b. Madison, Hamilton, and Jay
7. What is the economic system of the United States?
   Answer: d. market economy
8. What is one thing Benjamin Franklin is famous for?
   Answer: c. He started the first free libraries in the United States.

Unit 3, Take the Test, Section 7C. Writing Vocabulary Dictation

Listen to each sentence. Then, listen again and write what you hear.

1. We have freedom of speech in the United States.
2. A citizen has the right to vote.
3. The Constitution is the supreme law of the land.
4. The Bill of Rights is the first ten amendments.

Unit 4, Take the Test, Section 7A. Multiple Choice Questions.
Listen to the questions. Circle the correct answers.

1. What lands did the United States buy in 1803?
2. Name one of the two longest rivers in the United States.
3. Name the U.S. war between the North and the South.
4. Name one problem that led to the Civil War.
5. What group of people was taken to America and sold as slaves?
6. What did the Emancipation Proclamation do?
7. Which president freed the slaves?
8. What is another name for the Civil War?

CD 1

Track 11

Unit 4, Take the Test, Section 7B.
Now, listen again and check your answers.

1. What lands did the United States buy in 1803?
   Answer: c. Louisiana Territory
2. Name one of the two longest rivers in the United States.
   Answer: a. Mississippi River
3. Name the U.S. war between the North and the South.
   Answer: c. Civil War
4. Name one problem that led to the Civil War.
   Answer: b. slavery
5. What group of people was taken to America and sold as slaves?
   Answer: d. Africans
6. What did the Emancipation Proclamation do?
   Answer: d. freed the slaves in the Confederate states
7. Which president freed the slaves?
   Answer: a. Abraham Lincoln
8. What is another name for the Civil War?
   Answer: d. the War between the North and the South

CD 1

Track 12

Unit 4, Take the Test, Section 7C. Writing Vocabulary Dictation
Listen to each sentence. Then, listen again and write what you hear.

1. Lincoln's birthday is February 12.
2. The Civil War was between the North and the South.
3. Presidents' Day is in February.
4. Canada is north of the United States.
5. Mexico is south of the United States.

Unit 5, Take the Test, Section 7A. Multiple Choice Questions.

Listen to the questions. Circle the correct answers.

1. What did Susan B. Anthony do?
2. Which countries were our enemies during World War II?
3. What was the main concern of the United States during the Cold War?
4. Who was Dr. Martin Luther King, Jr.?
5. What movement tried to end racial discrimination?
6. Name one war fought by the United States in the 1900s.
7. Who was president during World War I?
8. What event happened in the United States on September 11, 2001?

Unit 5, Take the Test, Section 7B.

Now, listen again and check your answers.

1. What did Susan B. Anthony do?
   Answer: c. She fought for women's rights.
2. Which countries were our enemies during World War II?
   Answer: d. Germany, Japan, and Italy
3. What was the main concern of the United States during the Cold War?
   Answer: b. Communism
4. Who was Dr. Martin Luther King, Jr.?
   Answer: b. a Civil Rights leader
5. What movement tried to end racial discrimination?
   Answer: a. the Civil Rights movement
6. Name one war fought by the United States in the 1900s.
   Answer: d. World War I
7. Who was president during World War I?
   Answer: a. Woodrow Wilson
8. What event happened in the United States on September 11, 2001?
   Answer: b. Terrorists attacked the United States.

Unit 5, Take the Test, Section 7C. Writing Vocabulary Dictation

Listen to each sentence. Then, listen again and write what you hear.

1. We are all free in the United States.
2. Columbus Day is in October.
3. There are 50 states.
4. Many people died on September 11, 2001.

Unit 6, Take the Test, Section 7A. Multiple-Choice Questions
Listen to the questions. Circle the correct answers.

1. What do we show loyalty to when we say the Pledge of Allegiance?
2. Why does the flag have 13 stripes?
3. Why does the flag have 50 stars?
4. What is the name of the national anthem?
5. When do we celebrate Independence Day?
6. Name two national U.S. holidays.
7. What do we celebrate on Veterans Day?
8. On which holiday do we honor working people?

Unit 6, Take the Test, Section 7B.
Now, listen and check your answers.

1. What do we show loyalty to when we say the Pledge of Allegiance?
   Answer: b. the United States
2. Why does the flag have 13 stripes?
   Answer: b. because there were 13 original colonies
3. Why does the flag have fifty stars?
   Answer: a. one for each state in the country
4. What is the name of the national anthem?
   Answer: b. "The Star-Spangled Banner"
5. When do we celebrate Independence Day?
   Answer: a. July 4
6. Name two national U.S. holidays.
   Answer: c. Memorial Day and Labor Day
7. What do we celebrate on Veterans Day?
   Answer: a. We honor all U.S. veterans.
8. On which holiday do we honor working people?
   Answer: d. Labor Day

Unit 6, Take the Test, Section 7C. Writing Vocabulary Dictation
Listen to each sentence. Then, listen again and write what you hear.

1. The American flag is red, white, and blue.
2. The United States has 50 states.
3. Memorial Day is the last Monday in May.
4. The United States flag has thirteen stripes.
5. Flag Day is in June.

CD 1
Track 19

Unit 7, Take the Test, Section 7A. Multiple Choice Questions.
Listen to the questions. Circle the correct answers.

1. What is the legislative branch of government?
2. What are the two parts of the U.S. Congress?
3. How many U.S. senators are there?
4. The House of Representatives has how many voting members?
5. Why do some states have more representatives than other states?
6. Who makes federal laws?
7. What stops one branch of government from becoming too powerful?
8. Who vetoes bills?

CD 1
Track 20

Unit 7, Take the Test, Section 7B.
Now, listen again and check your answers.

1. What is the legislative branch of government?
   Answer: c. Congress
2. What are the two parts of the U.S. Congress?
   Answer: a. the Senate and the House of Representatives
3. How many U.S. senators are there?
   Answer: b. 100
4. The House of Representatives has how many voting members?
   Answer: d. 435
5. Why do some states have more representatives than other states?
   Answer: b. because they have more people
6. Who makes federal laws?
   Answer: c. Congress
7. What stops one branch of government from becoming too powerful?
   Answer: d. checks and balances
8. Who vetoes bills?
   Answer: b. the president

CD 1
Track 21

Unit 7, Take the Test, Section 7C. Writing Vocabulary Dictation
Listen to each sentence. Then, listen again and write what you hear.

1. The Congress meets in the Capitol Building.
2. There are two senators from each state.
3. The Congress makes the laws in the United States.
4. Washington, D.C. is the capital of the United States.
5. There are 100 senators.
6. Citizens elect their senators and representatives.

CD 2
Track 1

Unit 8, Take the Test, Section 7A. Multiple Choice Questions.
Listen to the questions. Circle the correct answers.

1. What is the executive branch of our government?
2. Who is in charge of the executive branch?
3. What are two cabinet-level positions?
4. How many Supreme Court justices are there?
5. What does the judicial branch do?
6. In what month do we vote for president?
7. What is the highest court in the United States?
8. Where does the president live and work?

CD 2
Track 2

Unit 8, Take the Test, Section 7B.
Now, listen again and check your answers.

1. What is the executive branch of our government?
   Answer: a. the president, vice president, cabinet, and departments
2. Who is in charge of the executive branch?
   Answer: c. the president
3. What are two cabinet-level positions?
   Answer: a. and c. Secretary of Agriculture and Secretary of Labor
4. How many Supreme Court justices are there?
   Answer: d. nine
5. What does the judicial branch do?
   Answer: a. reviews and explains the laws
6. In what month do we vote for president?
   Answer: b. November
7. What is the highest court in the United States?
   Answer: c. the Supreme Court
8. Where does the president live and work?
   Answer: a. the White House

CD 2
Track 3

Unit 8, Take the Test, Section 7C. Writing Vocabulary Dictation
Listen to each sentence. Then, listen again and write what you hear.

1. The president lives in the White House.
2. Washington, D.C., is the capital of the United States.
3. The president is elected in November.
4. Alaska is the largest state.
5. I want to live in the United States.

176 ★ Appendix C

Unit 9, Take the Test, Section 7A. Multiple Choice Questions.

Listen to the questions. Circle the correct answers. Fill in the information about your city and state.

1. What is the chief executive of a state government called?
2. What is one power of the states?
3. What is the chief executive of a city called?
4. Who is the governor of our state?
5. Who is the chief executive of our local government?
6. What is the capital of our state?
7. What is one power of our local government?
8. What is the highest court in our state?

Unit 9, Take the Test, Section 7B.

Now, listen again and check your answers.

1. What is the chief executive of a state government called?
   Answer: b. governor
2. What is one power of the states?
   Answer: b. to provide schooling and education
3. What is the chief executive of a city called?
   Answer: a. mayor
4. Who is the governor of our state?
   Answer: The governor of our state is _____ .
5. Who is the chief executive of our local government?
   Answer: The chief executive of our local government is _____ .
6. What is the capital of our state?
   Answer: The capital of our state is _____ .
7. What is one power of our local government?
   Answer: a. to provide health-care services
8. What is the highest court in our state?
   Answer: The highest court in our state is _____ .

Unit 9, Take the Test, Section 7C. Writing Vocabulary Dictation

Listen to each sentence. Then, listen again and write what you hear. Fill in the information about your city and state.

1. I live in _____ .
2. The vice president lives in Washington, D.C.
3. The mayor of this city is _____ .
4. The governor of this state is _____ .
5. Delaware was the first state in this country.
6. Why did you come to the United States?

Unit 10, Take the Test, Section 7A. Multiple Choice Questions.

Listen to the questions. Circle the correct answers.

1. What Immigration and Naturalization form is used to apply to become a naturalized citizen?
2. What is one responsibility that is only for U.S. citizens?
3. What is one right only for U.S. citizens?
4. What are two ways that Americans can participate in their democracy?
5. When is the last day you can send in federal income tax forms?
6. When must all men register for the Selective Service?
7. You must be _____ years old or older to become a naturalized citizen.
8. What is the literacy requirement?

Unit 10, Take the Test, Section 7B.

Now, listen again and check your answers.

1. What Immigration and Naturalization form is used to apply to become a naturalized citizen?
   Answer: c. N-400
2. What is one responsibility that is only for U.S. citizens?
   Answer: a. serve on a jury
3. What are two rights only for U.S. citizens?
   Answer: b. vote in a federal election and apply for a federal job
4. What are two ways that Americans can participate in their democracy?
   Answer: a. and b. Join a community group and vote.
5. When is the last day you can send in federal income tax forms?
   Answer: b. April 15
6. When must all men register for the Selective Service?
   Answer: c. at the age of 18
7. You must be _____ years old or older to become a naturalized citizen.
   Answer: b. 18
8. What is the literacy requirement?
   Answer: speak, You must understand, speak, read, and write simple English.

Unit 10, Take the Test, Section 7C. Writing Vocabulary Dictation

Listen to each sentence. Then, listen again and write what you hear.

1. What colors are in the American flag?
2. Do you have a one-dollar bill?
3. California has the most people of any state.
4. Labor Day is in September.
5. How long have you lived here?

CD 2
Tracks 10–17

The audio script for the 100 Civics (History and Government) Questions for the Redesigned Naturalization Test can be found in Appendix B, pages 133–142.

CD 2
Track 18

America the Beautiful by Katharine Lee Bates

O beautiful for spacious skies,
For amber waves of grain,
For purple mountain majesties
Above the fruited plain!
America! America!
God shed His grace on thee,
And crown thy good with brotherhood
From sea to shining sea!

CD 2
Track 19

The Star-Spangled Banner by Francis Scott Key

Oh, say, can you see,
by the dawn's early light,
What so proudly we hailed
at the twilight's last gleaming.
Whose broad stripes and bright stars,
through the perilous fight,
O'er the ramparts we watched,
were so gallantly streaming!
And the rocket's red glare,
the bombs bursting in air,
Gave proof through the night
that our flag was still there:
Oh, say, does that star-spangled
banner yet wave
O'er the land of the free
and the home of the brave?

CD 2
Track 20

The Pledge of Allegiance

I pledge allegiance to the flag
of the United States of America,
and to the republic for which it stands,
one nation, under God, indivisible,
with liberty and justice for all.

Photo Credits